NO

COMMENT!

...AND DON'T QUOTE ME ON THAT

To
Pauline
with best wishes

April 2021

NO
COMMENT!

...AND DON'T QUOTE ME ON THAT

from the sublime to the hilarious...
over 40 years of reporting
from the United Nations

THALIF DEEN

RODERICGRIGSON.COM

INTRODUCTION

In my 40-year journalistic career at the United Nations, I gained notoriety as a raconteur, a teller of tales, including tall tales. My beloved and caring wife, Lucille, who was a relentless source of inspiration for this book, never ceased to pummel me with two questions: "When are you writing your memoirs? What are you leaving behind for posterity?"

I was quick to respond with good-humored grace, as I usually do, this time with an anecdote attributed to one of my favorite comedians, the irrepressible Groucho Marx. When Groucho was once asked what he has done for posterity, he shot back: "Why should I? What has posterity done for me?"

I frequently used Lucille as a sounding board for my dry sense of newsroom humor. When a British Labor politician, Michael Foot, was appointed to chair a committee on nuclear disarmament in Europe, back in 1986, the London Times ran with one of its memorable headlines: FOOT HEADS ARMS BODY, we shared a laugh.

While appreciating my humor, Lucille was also a constructive critic, plus a travelling companion during most of my reportorial assignments covering international conferences in over 50 cities – extending from Rome to Reykjavik and from Stockholm to San Jose.

Asked when I plan to retire, I wise-cracked, "I am too old to retire."

And thereby hangs another tall tale!

thalif deen
New York,
February 2021

CHAPTER 1

The UN General Assembly in session. Credit: UN Photo/Manuel Elias

Where do UN Diplomats Hide During Politically Sensitive Voting?

The United Nations, created in 1945 following the devastation caused by World War II, was mandated with one central mission: the maintenance of international peace and security. But the 76-year-old Organization and its affiliated bodies – including the 193-member General Assembly and the 15-member Security Council— take decisions mostly by open voting, and few, by secret ballot.

But the seriousness of the UN's far-reaching mandate has been tempered by occasional moments of levity which have rocked the Glass House by the East River –- with laughter. The UN is a rich source of anecdotes—both real and apocryphal – in which the General Assembly (UNGA), the UN's highest policy-making body, takes center stage, along with the Security Council (UNSC) as a political sidekick.

When UN ambassadors and delegates congregate in the cavernous General Assembly hall at voting time, they have one of three options: either vote for, against or abstain.

The most intriguing, however, is a fourth option: to be suddenly struck with an urge to rush to the toilet. The frantic attempt to leave your seat vacant – and consequently, be counted as "absent" – takes place whenever the issue is politically sensitive.

When delegates are unable to vote with their conscience – don't want to incur the wrath of mostly Western aid donors or are taken unawares with no specific instructions from their capitals – they flee their seats.

At a lunch for reporters in his townhouse bordering Park Avenue in Manhattan, ("this was once owned by Gucci, now owned by Fulci"), Ambassador Francesco Paolo Fulci, an Italian envoy with a sharp sense of humor, described the fourth option as the "toilet factor" in UN voting.

And he jokingly suggested that the only way to resolve the problem is to install portable toilets in the back of the General Assembly hall so that delegates can still cast their votes while contemplating on their toilet seats. But for obvious reasons, there were no takers.

Regrettably, the UN's voting habits were not recorded when the world body commemorated the "International Year of Sanitation" in 2008, highlighting the fact that roughly 2.6 billion people worldwide do not have access to toilets or basic sanitation. Not surprisingly, UN delegates were excluded from that collective head count because the Secretariat never ran out of toilets. But the joke lingered on.

In most instances, the various regional groups and coalitions—including the Organization of Islamic Cooperation (OIC), the Group of 77, the Latin American and Caribbean States, the African Union (AU) and the Western European and Others (WEOG)— take decisions behind closed doors ahead of voting. But even though the "herd mentality" continues in most UN voting, there are rare occasions of an unscheduled vote taking delegates by surprise.

In the 1970s and 80s, the 116-member Non-Aligned Movement (NAM), founded in Belgrade in 1961, was one of the largest and most powerful political coalitions at the UN-led by countries such as Yugoslavia, India, Egypt, Ghana, Indonesia, Zambia, Cuba, and Sri Lanka.

As a general rule, all 116 countries vote in unison on General Assembly resolutions rarely breaking ranks. A Sri Lankan ambassador once recounted a message transmitted from his Foreign Ministry in Colombo – primarily directed at newly-arrived delegates which read – "If you are faced with an unscheduled surprise vote, and do not have any instructions from the Foreign Ministry, look to the right to see how

Yugoslavia is voting and look to the left to see how India is voting. If both ambassadors are seen bolting from their seats, just follow them to the toilet".

But NAM was a political powerhouse in the 1970s and 80s. Still, when Sri Lankan President J.R. Jayewardene (JRJ) inherited the chairmanship in February 1978, he was skeptical of NAM which was known to be politically independent, with no strong links to either of the world's two superpowers at that time, namely the US and the Soviet Union, who were engaged in a longstanding and bitter Cold War.

In an interview with an American news reporter, JRJ downgraded the political myth about "non-alignment" when he infamously declared there were only two "non-aligned countries" in the world: the US and the Soviet Union. All other countries, he argued, were politically aligned either with the US or the Soviets. The quote was apparently off- the-record and not-for attribution, but the reporter couldn't resist the temptation of running with it.

In September 1979, when JRJ handed over the chairmanship of NAM to Cuba at a summit meeting in Havana, the Western world and the mainstream media never accepted the fact that a strong pro-Soviet ally like Havana could ever be a "non-aligned" country.

As a result, right throughout Cuba's chairmanship of NAM (1979-1983), the New York Times, perhaps as part of its editorial policy, never wavered describing NAM as a "so-called Non-Aligned Movement" in every news story published in the paper. The "so-called" label was dropped only when India took over the chairmanship of NAM in 1983.

When "non-alignment" was a political buzz word, and NAM was in full swing, a UN diplomat once recounted the economic progress in Yugoslavia which had produced the Yugo, a small hatchback that arrived in United States in the late 1980s and early 1990s.

According to a report in the New York Times, the Yugo was said to be the first car from a Communist country to reach the American market. Equipped with front-wheel drive and a 55-horsepower engine, it sold at a base price of about $3,990, one of the cheapest in the market. But when scores of cars kept breaking down in the streets of New York, the Yugo was dubbed "an unaligned car from a non-aligned country." A political twist perhaps planted by the American automobile industry.

The only thing missing was a bumper sticker which should have read: "The parts falling off this car were made of the finest Yugoslav steel" (a parody of a quote once attributed to a motorist with his broken-down British-made car).

Meanwhile, long after the end of the Cold War, some of NAM's political mandate remained valid, including nuclear disarmament, the right to self-determination, the protection of national sovereignty, and the elusive goal a Palestinian homeland.

Former UN Secretary-General Boutros Boutros-Ghali told a NAM summit meeting in Colombia in 1995: "At Bandung in 1955, the birth of non-alignment was an act of stunning, worldtransfixing boldness. International politics were fundamentally and forever transformed." As he pointed out, non-alignment derived its political force from a new principle: the principle of solidarity.

But US Ambassador to the UN Richard Holbrooke (1999-2001) tried an old tactic to break that solidarity: divide and rule. In one of his farewell addresses to the African Group at the UN, Holbrooke said: "I respectfully ask the African countries to reconsider their association with the Non-Aligned Movement. The Non-Aligned Movement is not Africa's friend at this point. Your goals and NAM's are not synonymous."

Holbrooke argued that Africa's voice was weakened because of its association with NAM. "I have not seen a single issue in which NAM positions actually benefited the African Group." The US envoy also said that NAM, the largest single political group at the United Nations, should either cease to exist as a separate caucus or merge with the Group of 77 (G-77) developing nations. The G-77, the largest single economic group at the United Nations, consists of 134 members - and most developing nations are members of both groups.

Holbrooke said that African nations "should consider distancing themselves from NAM". "So that you can protect African interests and not allow yourself to be pushed by less than ten radicalized States into positions that you don't need." Even after Holbrooke ceased to be the US ambassador, the US Mission to the UN decided to circulate his speech as a UN document of the General Assembly giving it official credence.

But NAM counter attacked. By a coincidence, the chair at that time was from Africa. So, it was left to the South African ambassador, in his capacity as chairman of NAM, to respond. Holbrooke's proposal, he said, was an insult to the entire membership of the Movement. "This attempt by a non-NAM member to prescribe to the African members of the Movement is, at best uninformed, or at worst, misguided, misleading and constitutes an affront to NAM members as a whole."

"The decision by the US Mission to publish the statement under the General Assembly agenda can only be seen as an attempt to question the legitimacy of NAM," South African Ambassador Dumisani Shadrack Kumalo said. In a letter to NAM members, Kumalo said: "For our people, NAM will always be remembered for having stood steadfast in support of our struggle against apartheid whilst many outside NAM were either complacent or supportive of the racist regime of our past," he declared.

In the US State Department Holbrooke was known for his passionate pursuit of the US political agenda and never taking no for an answer. When Hillary Clinton was Secretary of State, he would pursue her in and out of office until she provided him with an answer or concurred with his view.

In a rare achievement, he held the position of Assistant Secretary of State for two different regions of the world (Asia from 1977-1981 and Europe from 1994-1996). Later, he was also the US Special Representative to Afghanistan and Pakistan (2009–10) under the Obama administration.

When Holbrooke was rushed to the hospital with an aneurysm in his heart had burst, ripping a hole in his aorta, the physician at the hospital told him to relax. "I can't relax", he told the doctor, "I am in charge of Afghanistan and Pakistan", two of the most politically troubled countries in the region. Three days later he died.

At the memorial service for Holbrooke in Washington DC in January 2011, Clinton recounted an incident when she was visiting Pakistan and Holbrooke would chase her around seeking her approval for one of his proposals on Afghanistan. At one point, Clinton told him: "Richard, do you realize you are in a woman's toilet in Pakistan". And there was loud laughter during the sober memorial ceremony.

In Pakistan, Clinton was apparently warned, that despite millions of dollars in economic and military aid to Islamabad, there were some elements in the government secretly supporting anti-American militant groups. She responded with a great quote: "You can't keep snakes in your backyard and only expect them to bite your neighbors."

CHAPTER 2

Secretary-General António Guterres briefing journalists.
At left is his Spokesman Stéphane Dujarric. UN Photo/Manuel Elias

"No Comment," says a Tight-Lipped UN Diplomat, "And Don't Quote Me on That."

For scores of journalists covering the UN for their newspapers thousands of miles away from home, one of the most coveted datelines was "Reporting from the United Nations."

Some of these correspondents come from developing nations, including India, Indonesia, Egypt, Brazil, Malaysia, Bosnia, Singapore, Sri Lanka, Pakistan, Saudi Arabia, and Lebanon, while others came from the Western world, including Italy, France, Germany, UK, and the US, plus Russia and China.

Besides reporting on military conflicts, civil wars, genocide, and war crimes in some of the world's political hotspots, most UN correspondents were also gifted raconteurs who could spin a tale or two.

The late Dharam Shourie, UN Bureau Chief for the Indian news agency, Press Trust of India (PTI), pointed out that journalists back home, in the 1950s and 1960s, could rarely afford the luxury of a tape recorder. So, most interviews, particularly with politicians and government bureaucrats, were either one-on-one or over the phone.

But if the interview got a strong blowback, politicians were quick to deny the entire story or falsely accuse the reporter of either misquoting or concocting the quotes. Unfortunately, journalists had no proof to nail the lying politicians.

According to Shourie, there was a rare instance in the 1960s when a reporter, armed with a bulky tape recorder, went to interview an Indian politician. The politician asked the reporter: "What is it that you are carrying". Told it was a tape recorder, he said: "No tape recorders here. Leave it outside my office." And added the punchline: "You are trying to deny me, my right to deny, what I am going to tell you."

Shourie also told me about inviting a visiting journalist, a rigid vegetarian, and a Brahmin Hindu, for lunch at the UN cafeteria. When he saw him serving himself beef stroganoff, Shourie was surprised and asked him: "I thought you were a strict vegetarian and did not eat beef." "Oh," said the visiting journalist: "I don't eat Indian cows, but I can eat American cows".

Meanwhile, journalists, rarely if ever, were able to get any on-the-record comments or reactions from ambassadors, diplomats, and senior UN officials because most of them followed the advice given to Brits during war time censorship in the UK: "Be like Dad, Keep Mum".

As Winston Churchill once remarked: "Diplomacy Is the art of telling people 'to go to hell' in such a way that they ask for directions." But as a general rule, most ambassadors and diplomats did not tell us either to go to hell or heaven – but avoided all comments on politically sensitive issues with the standard non-excuse:" Sorry, we have to get clearance from our capital".

But that "clearance" from their respective foreign ministries never came. Still, it was hard to beat a response from a tight-lipped Asian diplomat who told me: "No comment" – and as an after-thought, added: "And Don't Quote Me on That".

And most senior UN officials, on the other hand, never had even the basic courtesy or etiquette to respond to phone calls or email messages even with an acknowledgement. The lines of communications were mostly dead.

When I complained to the media-savvy Shashi Tharoor, a former Under-Secretary-General for Public Information and a one-time journalist and prolific author, he was explicit in his response when he said that every UN official – "from an Under-Secretary-General to a window-washer"—has the right to express an opinion in his or her area of expertise. But that rarely or ever happened.

A Brazilian diplomat once gave me an exclusive insider story, but warned it was "not for attribution and strictly off the record". But being familiar with the New York City's cultural scene, he added: "Off, Off the record. Like Off, Off-Broadway."

But there were exceptions: When IPS launched its daily conference newspapers, beginning with the 1982 Earth Summit in Rio, we were desperately chasing diplomats to get a sense of what was going on, mostly behind closed-doors, with the 134-member Group of 77, the largest single coalition of developing nations, expressing disappointment at the absence of any major pledges for funding.

As I was doing a wrap-up of the two-week-long conference, I approached Dr Gamani Corea, a former Secretary-General of the UN Conference on Trade and Development (UNCTAD) and a member of the Sri Lanka delegation, for a final comment. "We negotiated", he said with a tinge of sarcasm, "the size of the zero", as he held out his fingers to indicate the zero.

At IPS, where we focused on analytical pieces and not breaking news stories, our editors insisted on at least two of three sources quoted by name. Rarely did we attribute quotes – which at times sounded fictitious—to unnamed "Asian, Western, African or Third World diplomats".

When we ran an internship program – with most of the interns coming from US universities and also from Germany, Italy, Sweden, Brazil, Spain, India, Sri Lanka, Australia, Indonesia, UK and the Netherlands—I would cite a New Yorker cartoon where the wicked Queen, in the Snow White fairy tale, would stand before her magic mirror and ask: "Mirror, Mirror on the Wall, who is the Fairest of Them all?"—"And I want two sources quoted by name." And I would also repeat a piece of advice given in Journalism school: "Even if your mother says she loves you, double-check the story."

I also advised our interns of how crucial the lead para was in any news story—with would-be journalists spending weeks or months in journalism schools trying to crank out the perfect lead (or as the Americans call it the "lede").

I quoted the demanding editor (Walter Matthau) in the 1974 Billy Wilder classic "The Front Page" (there were three remakes of it) who berates his reporter (Jack Lemmon) for missing the fact that his fictional newspaper "The Examiner" had landed a scoop in tracking down a killer. Matthau complains he doesn't see this in the lead while Lemmon responds that it was in the second para. An indignant Matthau shouts back: "Who the hell reads the second para (in a news story)?"

When I discussed some of the great newspaper headlines, I told my interns about one such legendary headline in the London Times in 1986 when a British Labor party politician Michael Foot was appointed to chair a committee to look into nuclear disarmament in Europe. The classic headline read: FOOT HEADS ARMS BODY. And a legend was born.

I also told my interns there was a longstanding myth that journalists can do no wrong – and newspaper editors back home usually have the last word responding to any denials of a published news item: "We stand by our story" or "This correspondence is now closed".

Still, I remember reading an anecdote about a newspaper in a small town in mid-West USA which erroneously ran an obituary of an ailing town official in the "Deaths" columns. The indignant official called the newspaper editor from his hospital bed to confirm he was still alive and kicking—and demanding a retraction. "I am sorry", said the editor," We usually do not carry any corrections, but we can list your name under our "Births" column tomorrow".

Tarzie Vittachi, a renowned Sri Lankan newspaper editor and one-time deputy executive director of the UN children's agency UNICEF, once recounted the story of an African diplomat who sought his help to get coverage in the US media for his prime minister's address to the General Assembly.

The diplomat, a friend of Vittachi's, said the visiting African leader was planning to tell the world body his success stories in battling poverty, hunger, and HIV/AIDS. "How can I get this story into the front pages of US newspapers?" he asked, rather naively.

Vittachi, then a columnist and contributing editor to Newsweek magazine, jokingly retorted: "Shoot him – and you will get the front page of every newspaper in the US" As the old tabloid journalistic axiom goes: "If it bleeds, it leads."

Meanwhile, there were also sharp-witted journalists among the UN press corps, mostly members of the UN Correspondents'

Association (UNCA), representing journalists from over 70 countries.

When a Southeast Asian ambassador hosted a lunch for journalists, including the New York Times, the Wall Street Journal, and the Washington Post, among others, he told us there was a reason for the lunch. "We will soon begin our two-year term as a non-permanent member of the Security Council – and we need your cooperation (read: news coverage)".

And then added: "Hey guys, remember, as the Americans say, there is no such thing as a free lunch". A wise-cracking British journalist quipped: "Ambassador, there is also no such thing as a free press".

Still, there was at least one senior UN official with an off-beat sense of humor who once recounted an incident – but insisted it should be "strictly off the record" lest he be accused of male chauvinism".

He said he was speaking at a press conference in Europe to launch a UN report when following the briefing, several journalists, as they often do, rushed to the podium with more questions or seeking exclusive quotes. "There was this young buxom European woman reporter," he said, "who approached me with a label pinned to her chest which read: PRESS". And I did not know what to do".

CHAPTER 3

When UN Elections were Tainted by Bribery, Cheque Book Diplomacy & Luxury Cruises

When UN member states compete for the presidency of the General Assembly or membership in the Security Council or various UN bodies, the voting was largely tainted by bribery, cheque-book diplomacy and offers of luxury cruises in Europe – while promises of increased aid to the world's poorer nations came mostly with heavy strings attached.

In a bygone era, voting was by a show of hands, particularly in committee rooms. Still, in later years, a more sophisticated electronic board, high up in the General Assembly Hall, tallied the votes or in the case of elections to the Security Council or the International Court of Justice, the voting as by secret ballot.

In one of the hard-fought elections many moons ago, there were rumors that an oil-soaked Middle Eastern country was doling out high-end, Swiss-made wristwatches and stocks in the former Arabian-American Oil Company (ARAMCO), one of the world's largest oil companies, to UN diplomats as a trade-off for their votes.

So, when hands, both from right-handed and left-handed delegates, went up at voting time in the Committee room, the largest number of hands raised in favor of the oil-blessed candidate sported Swiss watches. As anecdotes go, it symbolized the corruption that prevails in voting in inter-governmental organizations, including the United Nations – perhaps much like most national elections the world over.

Just ahead of an election for membership in the Security Council, one Western European country offered free Mediterranean luxury cruises in return for votes while another country dished out –- openly in the General Assembly hall— boxes of gift-wrapped expensive Swiss chocolates.

So, it wasn't surprising that the Ambassador of a middle-income developing country, who kept losing successive elections, jokingly told his Foreign Ministry officials: "Let's stop running for elections until we can practice the fine art of stuffing ballot boxes –- as we do back home."

An age-old anecdote doing the rounds at the UN in the 1980s was characteristically male chauvinist. When a lady says no, she means maybe, when she says maybe, she means yes – and when she says yes, she is no lady. But election time at the UN is no better – simply because diplomatic double talk is a way of life in an institution where hopes are shattered by false promises.

When diplomats say maybe, they probably mean no, when they say yes, they mean maybe – and when they eventually say no, the message is transmitted via secret ballot.

If you don't read the right signals way ahead of the polls, and if your numbers don't add up, the best strategy is an exit strategy.

Fathulla Jameel, a former UN Ambassador and later Foreign Minister of the Maldives, recounted a story of how his resource-poor island nation, categorized by the UN as a Small Island Developing State (SID), would appeal to some of the richer nations to help fund some of the country's infrastructure projects.

At least one rich Asian country, a traditional donor, was the first to respond – and magnanimously too, he said. The project would be fully funded —free, gratis and for nothing. But there was a catch: "If there is a vote at the UN, and it is not of any national interest to your country", said the donor country's foreign ministry, "we would like to get your vote."

Perhaps for life – either the life of the Foreign Minister or the life of the island nation itself which was threatened with sea-level rise and in danger of being wiped off the face of the earth. The offer was a clever political payback. Development aid with no visible strings attached.

There was at least once instance when the president of the General Assembly, the highest policy-making body at the United Nations, was elected, on the luck of a draw - – following a dead heat.

With the Asian group failing to field a single candidate, the politically-memorable battle took place ahead of the 36th session of the General Assembly back in 1981 when three

Asian candidates contested the presidency: Ismat Kittani of Iraq, Tommy Koh of Singapore, and Kwaja Mohammed Kaiser of Bangladesh (described as the "battle of three Ks"—Kittani, Koh and Kaiser).

On the first ballot, Kittani got 64 votes; Kaiser, 46; and Koh, 40. Still, Kittani was short of a required majority — of the total number of members voting. On a second ballot, Kittani and Kaiser tied with 73 votes each (with 146 members present, and voting).

In order to break the tie, the outgoing General Assembly President – Rudiger von Wechmar of Germany – drew lots, as specified in Article 21 relating to the procedures in the election of the president (and as recorded in the Repertory of Practice of the General Assembly).

And the luck of the draw, based purely on chance, favored Kittani, in that unprecedented General Assembly election. But according to a joke circulating at that time, it was rumored that the flip of a coin decided the winner – but the tossed coin apparently had two heads and no tail.

In more recent years, however, the regional groups, including the Asian, African, Latin American, and Caribbean and the Western and Other Groups (WEOG) have called for a virtual ceasefire as they took turns according to the geographical rotation. The Groups would name their candidates who get elected without any opposition.

CHAPTER 4

A Security Council meeting in progress Credit: United Nations

US Spies Read Russian Lips in the Security Council Chamber

The United Nations, along with the 193 diplomatic missions located in New York, have long been veritable battlegrounds for spying, wire-tapping and electronic surveillance.

When the UN Correspondents Association (UNCA) held its annual award ceremony in December 2013, one of the video highlights was a hilarious skit on the clumsy attempts at spying going on inside the highest levels of the Secretariat—and right up to the 38th-floor offices of Secretary-General Ban Ki-moon.

When I took the floor, as one of the winners of the UNCA

gold medals, I gave the Secretary-General, standing next to me, an unsolicited piece of light-hearted advice: if you want to find out whether your phone line is being tapped, you only have to sneeze loudly, and a voice at the other end would instinctively and courteously respond: "Bless you", I said, amid laughter.

Perhaps by coincidence, three days later, the New York Times ran a story about the widespread electronic surveillance by the US National Security Agency (NSA) and Britain's spy agency, the Government Communications Headquarters (GCHQ), which had targeted over 1,000 political leaders, diplomats, and international institutions. These included the UN children's agency UNICEF and the Geneva-based U.N. Institute for Disarmament Research (UNIDIR).

At the UN, virtually all the big powers play the spying game, including the US, the Russians (and the Soviets during the Cold War era), the French, the Brits, and the Chinese — and none of them can afford to take a "holier than thou" attitude.

During the height of the Cold War in the 1960s and 1970s, the UN was a veritable battle ground for the United States and the now-defunct Soviet Union to spy on each other. The American and Soviet spooks were known to be crawling all over the building – in committee rooms, in the press gallery, in the Secretariat and, most importantly, in the UN library which was a drop-off point for sensitive political documents.

The extent of Cold War espionage in the United Nations was also laid bare by a 1975 US Congressional Committee, named after Senator Frank Church (Democrat-Idaho) who chaired it while investigating abuses by the Central Intelligence Agency (CIA), National Security Agency (NSA), Federal Bureau of Investigation (FBI), and the Internal Revenue Service (IRS).

The evidence given before the Church Committee included a revelation that the CIA had planted one of its Russian lip-reading experts in a press booth overlooking the Security Council chamber so that he could monitor the lip movements of Russian delegates, as they consulted each other in low whispers. Obviously, there was nothing sacred in the corridors of power at the United Nations.

In his 1978 book, "A Dangerous Place," Senator Daniel Patrick Moynihan, a former US envoy to the United Nations, described the cat-and-mouse espionage game that went on inside the bowels of the world body, and particularly the UN library.

Back in October 2013, When Clare Short, Britain's former minister for international development, revealed that British intelligence agents had spied on former UN Secretary-General Kofi Annan by bugging his office just before the disastrous US invasion of Iraq in March 2003, the UN chief was furious that his discussions with world leaders had been compromised.

And as she talked to Annan on the 38th floor of the UN Secretariat building, Short told the British Broadcasting Corporation (BBC), she was thinking, "Oh dear, there will be a transcript of this, and people will see what he and I are saying." Nearly 10 years later, the accusing finger was pointed towards the United States, not Britain.

James A. Paul, who monitored the politics of the United Nations for over 19 years as executive director of the New York-based Global Policy Forum, told IPS US electronic spying at the UN is a logical part of the worldwide espionage program by the US National Security Agency (NSA).

The program has come to light following documents released by Edward Snowden, a US whistleblower who was an NSA contractor, worked for the CIA and is currently living in political exile in Russia.

"It shows us the latest electronic approaches to surveillance 'listening', including the reports that the US has cracked into the UN's encrypted video system and that there is very aggressive monitoring of UN officials and high-ranking diplomats," he said.

Paul said none of this can be a surprise (though it is no less outrageous) in view of the tapping of the phones of 35 heads of state, including German Chancellor Angela Merkel, and the collection of information from some 70 million calls during one month in France.

"The UN has argued that surveillance targeting the organization is contrary to international law and to the US's responsibility as the host country, but such claims have been systematically and flagrantly disregarded," he noted.

Meanwhile, in April 1978, UN Under-Secretary-General Arkady Shevchenko of the then USSR had the dubious distinction of being the highest-ranking Soviet UN official to defect to the United States –-with bag, baggage, and a mistress, to boot.

Shevchenko, who was head of the UN's Department of Political and Security Council Affairs, was accused of being a double agent working for US intelligence while spying for the Soviets inside the United Nations.

Back in September 2013, Brazilian President Dilma Rousseff, throwing diplomatic protocol to the winds, launched a blistering attack on the United States for illegally infiltrating its communications network, surreptitiously intercepting phone calls, and breaking into the Brazilian Mission to the United Nations.

Departing from a longstanding tradition of closed-door diplomacy on bilateral disputes, she dropped a political bombshell on the Assembly hall overflowing with world leaders, foreign ministers, and ambassadors from 193 countries sitting in rapt silence.

Justifying her public criticism, she told delegates that the problem of electronic surveillance goes beyond a bilateral relationship. "It affects the international community itself and demands a response from it."

Rousseff said revelations concerning the activities of a global network of electronic espionage have caused indignation and repudiation in public opinion around the world. But in Brazil, she said, "The situation was even more serious, as it emerged that we were targeted by this intrusion."

She said that personal data of citizens was intercepted indiscriminately. Corporate information, often of high economic and even strategic value, was at the center of espionage activity. At the same time, Brazilian diplomatic missions, among them the Permanent Mission to the United Nations and the president's office, had their communications intercepted, she charged.

Rousseff unleashed her attack even as US President Barack Obama was awaiting his turn to address the General Assembly on the opening day of the annual high-level debate. By longstanding tradition, Brazil is the first speaker, followed by the United States.

Even though Obama, and the US, had the right of reply, he did not address the issues raised by Rousseff, who also canceled a proposed official visit to the White House protesting the electronic surveillance of her country. "We have let the US government know our disapproval, and demanded explanations, apologies and guarantees that such procedures will never be repeated," she said.

According to documents released by US whistleblower Edward Snowden, the illegal electronic surveillance of Brazil was conducted by the US National Security Agency (NSA). The Germany-based *Der Spiegel* magazine reported that NSA technicians had managed to decrypt the UN's internal video teleconferencing (VTC) system, as part of its surveillance of the world body.

The combination of this new access to the UN and the cracked encryption code led to "a dramatic improvement in VTC data quality and (the) ability to decrypt the VTC traffic," the NSA agents reportedly said. In the article, titled "How

America Spies on Europe and the UN", *Spiegel* said that in just under three weeks, the number of decrypted communications increased from 12 to 458.

Subsequently, there were new charges of spying --but this time around the Americans were accused of using the UN Special Commission (UNSCOM) in Baghdad to intercept Iraqi security intelligence in an attempt to undermine, and perhaps overthrow, the government of President Saddam Hussein.

The charges, spread across the front pages of the Washington Post and the Boston Globe, only confirmed the longstanding Iraqi accusation that UNSCOM was "a den of spies," mostly American and British.

Established by the Security Council immediately after the 1991 Gulf War, UNSCOM was mandated to eliminate Iraq's weapons of mass destruction and destroy that country's capabilities to produce nuclear, biological, and chemical weapons.

The head of UNSCOM, Richard Butler of Australia, however, vehemently denied charges that his inspection team in Iraq had spied for the United States. "We have never conducted spying for anyone," Butler told reporters. Asked to respond to news reports that UNSCOM may have helped Washington collect sensitive Iraqi information to destabilize the Saddam Hussein regime, Butler retorted: "Don't believe everything you read in print." But he never made the distinction between what was believable and what was unbelievable.

Around the same time, the New York Times weighed in with

a front-page story quoting US official as saying that "American spies had worked undercover on teams of UN arms inspectors ferreting out secret Iraqi weapons programmes." The cover, for all intents and purposes, had been blown. In an editorial, the Times said that "using UN activities in Iraq as a cover for American spy operations would be a sure way to undermine the international organization, embarrass the United States and strengthen Mr Hussein."

"Washington did cross a line it should not have if it placed American agents on the UN team with the intention of gathering information that could be used for military strikes against targets in Baghdad," the editorial said. The whole episode not only embarrassed the United Nations but also put its integrity, impartiality, and credibility in doubt.

CHAPTER 5

Dogs and Diplomats Not Welcome – Not Necessarily in that Order

When Ambassadors and other lower-ranking diplomats arrive in New York, most of them experience "culture shock" being forced to adjust to New York city living – including food, language, and apartment living.

In the 1970s, the Daily News recounted the story of a newly arrived diplomat from a conflict-ridden African country who was posted to New York – considered a safe-haven – following death threats against him by a rebel group in his home country. A few weeks after his arrival, he found a note slipped under his Manhattan apartment door with an ominous message: "The exterminator will be here tomorrow."

Panicked at the thought the rebel group had extended its reach, he was about to rush to the nearest police precinct when he accosted the clerk at the reception desk in the lobby who told him: "Sir, the exterminator will be here not to kill diplomats, but to exterminate roaches, bed bugs and mice." That was one of the first diplomatic lessons in Manhattan apartment living.

Meanwhile, some UN diplomats had an excruciating time signing leases for new apartments. The landlords who have had bitter experiences fighting tenants over unpaid rents and damages to their apartments avoided diplomats as tenants because they were safeguarded by diplomatic immunity and couldn't be dragged into Small Claims Court. So, at least on one building, the landlord apparently had a sign which read: "Dogs and Diplomats Not Welcome."

The UN community, on average, contributes a hefty $3.7 billion annually to the New York city economy generating over 25,000 jobs, according to a 2016 report from the Mayor's Office for International Affairs. But still, some politicians have a constant gripe against the UN, primarily because of its some-time anti-Israel and anti-US stand, or because of the misconceived notion that all UN personnel are entitled to diplomatic immunity and privileges. They are not – and some of the best things in life are certainly not duty-free.

Even successive New York city Mayors have occasionally unleashed their hatred and venom at the world body – even as the UN keeps pumping money into city coffers.

A former Mayor Ed Koch called the UN a "sewer". Mayor, Rudolph Giuliani, said he would not miss the UN if it decides to pack up and leave New York. But much of this rhetoric was political grandstanding.

The Iraqis, who were under a rigorous UN economic and

military embargo for nearly ten years, constantly complained they were facing sanctions from New York landlords. The Iraqi Mission to the UN said that some of its newly appointed delegates were forced to seek shelter in hotels because real estate agents in the UN neighborhood were ostracizing Iraqi diplomats.

When the United Nations decided to locate its secretariat in the city of New York, the United States as host nation signed a "headquarters agreement" back in 1947 not only ensuring diplomatic immunity to foreign diplomats but also pledging to facilitate the day-to-day activities of member states without any hindrance. But there were several instances of open violation of the agreement.

But back in January 2011, JP Morgan Chase Bank decided to close its division that serves diplomatic and foreign government missions has prompted a strong protest from member states. A letter sent by the bank advised all UN Missions to close their business accounts by Mar. 31.

Additionally, all business credit cards were also terminated by that date. A letter sent by the US Mission to the United Nations to the 192 member states pointedly referred to a "recent decision by large commercial banks (plural) to discontinue diplomatic or foreign government accounts." The implication was that more than one commercial bank – besides Chase – may be trying to throw out all diplomatic business accounts, virtually blacklisting them.

Although the Chase bank, in its letter to UN Missions, did

not officially give any reason for its sudden decision, one UN diplomat told IPS it was probably related to preventing money laundering and terrorism funding.

According to Section 17 of the Headquarters Agreement, "American authorities" were expected to "supply on equitable terms with the necessary public services", including telephone and telegraph facilities, to the United Nations and its member states.

"In case of any interruption or threatened interruption of any such services, the appropriate American authorities will consider the needs of the United Nations as being of equal importance with similar needs of essential agencies of the government of the United States, and will take steps accordingly, to ensure that the work of the United Nations is not prejudiced."

In a letter sent to all member states, the US Mission said it was aware that "the majority of the Permanent Missions in New York have for years been clients of JP Morgan Chase, and that the closure by the bank of this division means that the Mission's business accounts will likewise by closed by March 31."

The letter also said that some Missions "believe that they may experience difficulty in establishing accounts at other financial institutions in the New York area". Absolving the host country of any responsibility, the letter said JP Morgan Chase was a private sector bank, and its decisions are made for "business reasons alone". But those reasons remained unstated.

"The government of the United States has no authority to force banks to continue to serve their customers or to open or close any accounts," it said.

The United States, which is legally obliged to respect international diplomatic norms as host country to the United Nations, has also been accused of imposing unfair travel restrictions on UN diplomats in the country. Back in August 2000, the Russian Federation, Iraq and Cuba protested the "discriminatory" treatment, which they say targets countries that displease the US.

Pleading national security concerns, Washington has long placed tight restrictions on diplomats from several "unfriendly" nations, including those deemed "terrorist states," particularly Cuba, Iraq, Iran, North Korea, Sudan, Syria, and Libya. UN diplomats from these countries must obtain permission from the US State Department to travel outside a 25-mile radius from New York City.

US delegate Robert Moller said the term "national security" should not be taken lightly because it did not deal only with espionage. While he did not want to get into nitpicking over notifications, the US did not set up any impediments to UN-related business. Personal travel was the issue, he declared.

Responding to the letter, Moller struck a note of sarcasm when he said that while the US was "honored" that the Cuban ambassador wanted to travel in the United States, the key point was that the Town Hall Forum in Los Angeles was not a U.N.-sponsored event. The Cuban ambassador had no reason to be there, Moller added.

CHAPTER 6

Secretary-General Boutros Boutros-Ghali (1992-1996) Credit: UN Vienna

"If You want the Approval of France, You Must Not Only Speak French but also Speak English with a French Accent..."

When Egypt's onetime Foreign Minister Boutros Boutros-Ghali was running for the post of UN Secretary-General in late 1991, he had to contend with the candidature of Bernard Chidzero, then foreign minister of Zimbabwe.

As the campaign began to intensify, Boutros-Ghali recounted a brief encounter with Chidzero, a longstanding friend, at a conference in Africa, a continent which at that time claimed the job of UN chief based on geographical rotation.

Chidzero, who hailed from an English-speaking country and was backed by the UK and the 54-member Commonwealth of mostly ex-British colonies, was in conversation with Boutros-Ghali when he suddenly switched from English to French.

Having picked up the subtle message, Boutros-Ghali said he put his arms around Chidzero and jokingly remarked, "Bernard, if you want the approval of France, you must not only speak French but also speak English with a French accent."

France, a veto-wielding permanent member of the Security Council, has been so passionately protective of its language that it may well have exercised its veto on any candidate who did not speak French.

And no one who aspires to be the Secretary-General of the United Nations can expect to be elected to office if he or she does not have a working knowledge of French – or at least promises to eventually master the language – because France considers it the "language of international diplomacy".

Over the last 76 years, the two working languages of the United Nations have been primarily English and French, although there are four other official languages recognized by the world body: Chinese, Arabic, Spanish, and Russian.

Boutros-Ghali, who was fluent in English, Arabic and French, held "the world's most impossible job" from January 1992 through December 1996. Asked at a briefing with reporters about his fluency in three languages, Boutros-Ghali jokingly said his primary language was Arabic "because when I fight with my wife, I fight in Arabic."

The independence of the Secretary-General, he pointed out, is a longstanding myth perpetuated mostly outside the United Nations. As an international civil servant, he is expected to shed his political loyalties when he takes office, and more importantly, never seek or receive instructions from any governments.

But virtually every single Secretary-General—nine at last count – has played ball with the world's major powers in violation of Article 100 of the UN charter. Boutros-Ghali, the only Secretary-General to be denied a second term because of a negative US veto, unveiled the insidious political manoeuvring that goes inside the glass house.

The US, which preaches the concept of majority rule to the outside world, exercised its veto even though Boutros-Ghali had 14 of the 15 votes in the Security Council, including the votes of the other four permanent members of the Council, namely the UK, France, Russia and China.

In such circumstances, tradition would demand the dissenting US abstain on the vote and respect the wishes of the overwhelming majority in the Security Council. But the US refused to acknowledge the vibrant political support that Boutros-Ghali had garnered in the world body. When Kurt Waldheim of Austria (1972-1981) ran for an unprecedented third term as Secretary-General, he was reportedly vetoed 16 times until he withdrew his candidature, to be eventually succeeded by Javier Perez de Cuellar.

Unlike most of his predecessors and successors, Boutros-

Ghali refused to blindly play ball with the US even though he occasionally caved into US pressure at a time when Washington had gained a notoriety for trying to manipulate the world body to protect its national interests.

In his 368-page book titled "Unvanquished: A US-UN Saga" (Random House, 1999), he provided an insider's view of how the United Nations and its chief administrative officer (CAO) were manipulated by the Organization's most powerful member: The United States.

Although he was accused by Washington of being "too independent" of the US, he eventually did everything in his power to please the Americans. But still, the US was the only country to say "no" to a second five-year term for Boutros-Ghali.

In his book, Boutros-Ghali recalls a meeting in which he tells the then-Secretary of State Warren Christopher that many Americans had been appointed to UN jobs "at Washington's request over the objections of other UN member states." "I had done so, I said, because I wanted American support to succeed in my job (as Secretary-General"), Boutros-Ghali says. But Christopher refused to respond.

When he was elected Secretary-General in January 1992, Boutros-Ghali noted that 50 percent of the staff assigned to the UN's administration and management were Americans, although Washington paid only 25 percent of the UN's regular budget.

When the Clinton administration took office in Washington

in January 1993, Boutros-Ghali was signaled that two of the highest-ranking UN staffers appointed on the recommendation of the outgoing Bush administration – Under-Secretary-General Richard Thornburgh and Under-Secretary-General Joseph Verner Reed – were to be dismissed even though they were theoretically "international civil servants" answerable only to the world body.

They were both replaced by two other Americans who had the blessings of the Clinton Administration. Just before his election in November 1991, Boutros-Ghali remembers someone telling him that John Bolton, the US Assistant Secretary of State for International Organizations, was "at odds" with the earlier Secretary-General Javier Perez de Cuellar because he had "been insufficiently attentive to American interests."

"I assured Bolton of my serious regard for US policy." "Without American support," Boutros-Ghali told Bolton, "the United Nations would be paralyzed."

CHAPTER 7

United Nations Headquarters, New York: Credit: United Nations

A UN Secretariat Rising from the Remains of a Decrepit Slaughterhouse on First Avenue...

Back in the late 1990s, Senator Jesse Helms, a rightwing Republican from the US state of North Carolina, carried out a virulent one-person hate-campaign against the UN – and its very presence in New York.

A fulltime chairman of the powerful Senate Foreign Relations Committee – and a part-time UN basher—the late Helms publicly complained that providing funds to the UN is like "pouring money into a rathole". Helms wanted the "Glass House by the East River" shipped out of New York — for good.

The Senator magnanimously offered to host a farewell party for the United Nations if the world body agrees to leave New York — for good.

"I disagree with the premises upon which the United Nations is built and with the illusion that it propagates," Senator Jesse Helms, chairman of the powerful Senate Foreign Relations Committee, said in a letter to the World Federalist Association. "It would be one thing if the United Nations were just an international sideshow, but it plays a greater role. It is a vast engine for the promotion of socialism, and to promote this purpose, the US provides a quarter of its budget," he said.

Helms, one of the strongest opponents of the United Nations in the US Congress, said he has long called for "our country's departure from this Organization, and vice versa."

Charles Lichtenstein, a former US Deputy Permanent Representative to the UN Mission, once said he would urge members of the United Nations to move out of New York if they did not like the treatment they were receiving in the United States.

Helms — with tongue firmly entrenched in cheek — said he would join Lichtenstein in waving goodbye to all the UN member- states "as they sail away into the sunset."

Fast forward to 2017-2020

Since he took office back in January 2017, US President Donald Trump (2017-2020) either de-funded, withdrew from, or denigrated several UN agencies and affiliated institutions, including the World Health Organization (WHO), the UN Relief and Works Agency for Palestinian Refugees (UNRWA), the World Trade Organization (WTO), the UN Educational, Scientific and Cultural Organization (UNESCO), the UN Population Fund (UNFPA), the UN Human Rights Council and the International Criminal Court (ICC), among others.

Meanwhile, when the UN was scouting around for funds to build its headquarters in 1946, John D. Rockefeller Jr, a renowned American philanthropist, gifted $8.5 million for the construction of a 39-storeyed complex on a 16-acre piece of land which was home to a decrepit slaughterhouse.

Since the abattoir, also dubbed the "bull house", was such a monstrous eyesore, no one apparently wanted to live in the East Side neighborhood where the UN building now stands, and where both rents and property values were dismally low in the 1940s.

The UN was apparently convinced that the slaughterhouse compound would be an ideal location for the new headquarters. Never mind the blood and the killings—and certainly not for an institution which stood for harmony and world peace. But rumor has it that Rockefeller and his friends owned lots of property in the neighborhood. So, when the UN finished constructing its landmark building in 1952, property values began to skyrocket to unprecedented heights.

And all the property owners in the UN vicinity made out like bandits – raking in millions of dollars in rising property values and real estate earnings. As one Third World diplomat commented: "it was part philanthropy, part business acumen".

The scene shifts to the year 2000 as Donald Trump, a New York real estate mogul, and later US President, whose ego is as monumental as his high-storied buildings, constructed a massive residential complex in the shadow of the UN.

The 90-storeyed luxury apartment complex was apparently built, in violation of an undertaking given by the City of New York, that no building in the neighborhood would rise above the UN complex. But despite protests, including one from the UN, the skyscraper continued its journey upwards.

The prices in the Trump Tower ranged from $800,000 (for a one-roomed apartment) to $18 million for a penthouse. A primary reason for such unprecedented property values is the mere physical presence of the UN, one of the biggest tourist attractions in the city.

The UN Secretariat building, which underwent a multi-million-dollar renovation under a Capital Master Plan at a cost of over $1.9 billion, 2006 through 2014, is home to over 3,000, including staffers, journalists and diplomats who transition through its corridors every day. The refurbishment contract was signed In July 2007 with the subsidiary of a Swedish firm, Skanska USA Buildings

If the world's separatist movements wind up carving new nation-states - from Kashmir to Kurdistan – the UN could well house over 200 members, up from its present 193. As a result of the renovation, the General Assembly is physically ready for newly emerging nations.

Meanwhile, there is an age-old anecdote about a former Secretary-General driving into the UN compound with a friend who looks at the imposing 39-storeyed building and asks: How many people work here? "Only half", says the Secretary-General.

But when the right-wing, hardline conservative John Bolton was US Ambassador to the UN (2005-2006), he notoriously remarked: "There's no such thing as the United Nations. If the UN secretariat building in New York lost ten stories, it wouldn't make a bit of difference." The punchline, however, came from a New York Times columnist who said Bolton would do better as an urban planner than a US diplomat.

Whenever the General Assembly meets in the second week of September every year, the high-level debate is a platform for never-ending speeches by 193 world leaders, including prime ministers, presidents, and foreign ministers.

A memorable Soviet-US confrontation took place at the General Assembly hall in October 1960 during the height of the Cold War, but this time it was between the USSR and the Philippines, considered a close US ally at that time. The Filipino delegate Lorenzo Sumulong, lashed out at the USSR, pointing out that "the peoples of Eastern Europe and elsewhere (under Soviet domination) have been deprived of the free exercise of their civil and political rights and which have been swallowed up, so to speak, by the Soviet Union".

Incensed by the remark, the Soviet leader Nikita Khrushchev, who was leading the Soviet delegation, hit back with a vengeance, describing the Filipino as "a jerk, a stooge, and a lackey", and a "toady of American imperialism" –words that are rarely heard in the General Assembly or the Security Council these days. Forget the North Korean refrain: "Running Dogs of Imperialism".

But an equally legendary story was the longstanding rumor that Khrushchev removed his shoe and kept banging on his desk, to be recognized, on the point of order. According to one rumor, the shoe-banging never happened (and there were no UN photographers or cell phone cameras to record the incident for posterity or the UN archives). The only evidence was a single photo in circulation, which was dismissed by some as a fake concocted by US intelligence – and that was long before the age of digital technology and photo-shopping.

But according to another unconfirmed rumor, Khrushchev did bang his shoes – but the sole was riddled with holes, and the shoe was badly in need of urgent repairs. That was probably an anti-Soviet canard by the US or its allies, who claimed they were witnesses to the incident in the General Assembly hall

Meanwhile, a security officer once recalled an incident

where the prime minister from an African country, addressing the General Assembly, was heckled by a group of African students. As is usual with hecklers, the boisterous group was taken off the visitor's gallery, grilled, photographer and banned from entering the UN premises. But about five years later, one of the hecklers returned to the UN – this time, as foreign minister of his country, and addressed the world body.

There w as also a widespread r umor t hat an A merican political activist and civil rights leader, Andrew Young, was part of an anti-apartheid demonstration outside the UN in the 1960s. And about ten years later, he returned as the US Ambassador to the United Nations (1977-79) – proving that in politics and diplomacy, the wheel of fortune always keeps on turning.

CHAPTER 8

Ernesto "Che" Guevara, Minister of Industries of Cuba, addresses the General Assembly on Dec. 11, 1964. - UN Photo/TC

The Day Anti-Castro Forces Tried to Bomb the UN Building...

When the politically-charismatic Ernesto Che Guevara, once second-in-command to Cuban leader Fidel Castro, was at the United Nations to address the General Assembly sessions back in 1964, the UN headquarters came under attack – literally. The speech by the Argentine-born Marxist revolutionary was momentarily drowned by the sound of an explosion.

The anti-Castro forces in the United States, backed by the Central Intelligence Agency (CIA), had mounted an insidious campaign to stop Che Guevara from speaking. A 3.5-inch bazooka was fired at the 39-storeyed Secretariat building by the East River while a vociferous CIA-inspired anti-Castro, anti-Che Guevara demonstration was taking place outside the UN building on New York's First Avenue and 42nd street.

But the rocket launcher – which was apparently not as sophisticated as today's shoulder-fired missiles and rocket-propelled grenades – missed its target, rattled windows, and fell into the river about 200 yards from the building. One newspaper report described it as "one of the wildest episodes since the United Nations moved into its East River headquarters in 1952."

As longtime UN staffers would recall, the failed 1964 bombing of the UN building took place when Che Guevara launched a blistering attack on US foreign policy and denounced a proposed de-nuclearization pact for the Western hemisphere. It was one of the first known politically motivated terrorist attacks on the United Nations. After his Assembly speech, Che Guevara was asked about the attack aimed at him. "The explosion has given the whole thing more flavor," he joked, as he chomped on his Cuban cigar.

When he was told by a reporter that the New York City police had nabbed a woman, described as an anti-Castro Cuban exile, who had pulled out a hunting knife and jumped over the UN wall, intending to kill him, Che Guevara said: "It is better to be killed by a woman with a knife than by a man with a gun."

Over the years, the United States has routinely led or co-sponsored scores of UN resolutions critical of human rights violations in Cuba and consistently voted against every single

General Assembly resolution calling on Washington to lift the economic embargo on Havana imposed in 1960.

Cuba's Fidel Castro, who addressed the General Assembly on several occasions, was one of the last of the world's ever-lasting socialists and a steadfast Communist for all seasons. Neither the collapse of the Soviet Union in 1991 nor the triumph of capitalism over socialism in the post-Cold War era deterred Castro from abandoning his political and socialist ideals.

In the 1960s, the CIA pulled out virtually everything in its bag of dirty tricks to oust Castro – even making an attempt to surreptitiously introduce a chemical powder into his shoes so that his trademark beard would fall off making him "a laughingstock of the Communist world." But the redoubtable Castro survived them all – including a rigid US embargo imposed on his country which has all but crippled the economy.

During an April 2000 summit meeting of the Group of 77, it was Secretary-General Kofi Annan's turn to praise Castro, as he singled out Cuba as one of the few developing nations with "impressive" achievements in social development. Annan said that Cuba's achievements in health, education and literacy were all the more significant given the size of its domestic product per capita - and the suffering the country has undergone since the US-imposed economic embargo of July 1963.

As the UN's human development index (HDI) made clear, year after year, he said, "Cuba should be the envy of many other nations ostensibly far richer." Annan pointed out that Cuba's success does not alleviate the need for a global economic and political environment that is more conducive to the countries of the South. "But it does demonstrate how much nations can do with the resources they have if they focus on the right priorities - health, education and literacy," he added.

In October 2009, the administration of President Barack Obama, which had vowed to improve relations with sanctions-hit Cuba, refused to break away from the traditional stand taken by successive US governments and voted against a UN resolution calling for an end to the 47-year-old US economic, commercial, and financial embargo against the Caribbean island nation.

Of the then 192 member states, an overwhelming 187 voted in favor of the resolution (as against 185 the previous year), with only three against (the United States, Israel, and Palau), and two abstentions (Marshall Islands and Micronesia).

The US has continued to remain largely isolated in successive General Assembly votes on one of "the most enduring trade embargoes in history" imposed on Cuba back in 1962. The annual vote is routinely viewed as a political and moral victory for Cuba because diplomatic support for the United States has progressively declined over the years.

The Group of 77, the largest single coalition of developing nations, called on the United States to bring an end to the decades-old embargo and to fully adhere to the principles of mutual respect and non-interference in the internal affairs of a sisterly country. But, as of now, the US embargo continues.

CHAPTER 9

A view of the helicopter as it approached the North Lawn of the UN campus.
Credit: UN Photo/Michos Tzovaras

The Night Yasser Arafat, Facing Death Threats, Slept in a Make-Shift Bedroom in the Secretary-General's Office...

The Leader of the Palestine Liberation Organization (PLO), Yasser Arafat, arrived at UN Headquarters by helicopter on 13 November 1974. But Arafat was denied a US visa for a second visit to the UN in 1988.

When Arafat was denied the visa to visit New York to address the United Nations, the General Assembly defied the United States by temporarily moving the UN's highest policy-making body to Geneva – perhaps for the first time in UN history – providing a less-hostile political environment for the leader of the Palestine Liberation Organization (PLO).

Arafat, who first addressed the UN in 1974, took a swipe at Washington when he prefaced his statement by saying "it never occurred to me that my second meeting with this honorable Assembly, since 1974, would take place in the hospitable city of Geneva".

On his 1974 visit, he avoided the hundreds of pro and anti-Arafat demonstrators outside the UN building by arriving in a helicopter which landed on the North Lawn of the UN campus adjoining the East River. When he addressed the General Assembly, there were confusing reports whether or not Arafat carried a gun in his holster— "in a house of peace" – which was apparently not visible to delegates.

One news story said Arafat was seen "wearing his gun belt and holster and reluctantly removing his pistol before mounting the rostrum." "Today, I have come bearing an olive branch and a freedom-fighter's gun. Do not let the olive branch fall from my hand," he told the Assembly. But there were some delegates who denied Arafat carried a weapon.

Setting the record straight, Samir Sanbar, a former UN Assistant Secretary-General and head of the Department of Public Information told me it was discreetly agreed that Arafat would keep the holster while the gun was to be handed over to Abdelaziz Bouteflika, l ater F oreign Minister and President of Algeria (1999-2019).

The speech, drafted in Arabic by Palestinian poet Mahmoud Darwish, stressed the spelling in formal Arabic of the "green branch" which the PLO Chairman still misspelt.

Incidentally, when anti-Arafat New York protesters on First Avenue shouted: "Arafat Go Home", his supporters responded that was precisely what he wanted—a home for the Palestinians to go to.

Iftikhar Ali, a longstanding UN correspondent for the Associated Press of Pakistan (APP), who has covered General Assembly sessions since 1971, told me Arafat's helicopter landed on the UN's North Lawn was around 3 am.

Among those who received him was UN Chief of Protocol Aly Teymour of Egypt – whose father was chief of protocol for King Farouk – and who handled all arrangements for Arafat's stay overnight in the UN Secretariat because of security risks of putting him up in a New York hotel.

The helicopter carrying Arafat was the second to land – the first one was probably a decoy, Ali said. "There were some cameramen present at that unearthly hour and only two print media reporters – the late Tony Goodman of Reuters and me. Arafat was escorted by security men into the UN building and to the Secretary-General's 38th floor where he spent the night in a temporary bedroom".

But that bedroom had not been used for years, and the color of water was brown when the bathroom's faucet was opened. Mercifully, it was not an attempt by Israeli intelligence to poison the PLO leader.

There was also a legendary story of how Arafat, who was on an Israeli hit-list, never slept on the same bed on two consecutive nights – to outwit assassins trying to kill him in Israeli-occupied Palestinian territory.

Meanwhile, Palestine, which was never afforded the status of a full-fledged UN member state pulled off a coup when the 134-member Group of 77, the largest single political coalition at the UN, elected it as its chairman, back in 2018, much against US protests.

Nikky Haley, the vociferously anti-Palestine US Ambassador to the United Nations, warned member states she will "take down names" of those who vote against American interests in the world body-perhaps with the implicit threat of cutting US aid to countries that refuse to play ball with the diplomatically reckless Trump administration.

But that vengeance-driven headcount - and no ball playing - could be a tedious exercise for the US when 146 out of 193 member states voted in the General Assembly to affirm Palestine as the new chairman of the Group of 77. The 146 included some of the US's strongest Western allies, plus four of the five permanent members of the UN Security Council: UK, France, China, and Russia.

The only two countries that stood sheepishly by the US were Israel, its traditional client state, and Australia, a newcomer to the ranks of US supporters.

Although Arafat made it to the UN, some of the world's most controversial leaders, including Iraq's Saddam Hussein,

Syria's Hafez al-Assad and his son Bashar al-Assad, and North Korea's Kim il Sung and his grandson Kim Jong-un never made it to the UN.

Kul Gautam, a former UN Assistant Secretary-General and Deputy Executive Director of the UN children's agency UNICEF told me that another prominent world leader who never visited the UN nor addressed the General Assembly, was Egyptian President Hosni Mubarak. Although Mubarak visited Washington DC several times, he apparently NEVER visited New York, because of some unspecified special threat. "We at UNICEF learned this at the time of the 1990 World Summit for Children," he said.

Mubarak was one of the six initiating world leaders who convened the Summit for Children. "So, we expected him to personally attend and address the Summit. But we were surprised when the Egyptian government advised us, just a few days before the Summit, that its delegation would be headed by First Lady Suzanne Mubarak".

"That caused a serious protocol problem for us", said Gautam, because it had been agreed by the Summit Planning Committee, which included Egypt's Permanent Representative, Ambassador Amre Moussa, that only Heads of State or Government could attend & address the Summit.

"As Suzanne Mubarak was NOT a Head of State or Government, she could not sit at the same table as other HoS/HoG, nor address the Summit. So, we had to concoct all kinds of gymnastics to accommodate her," he said.

"We had a similar problem with Pakistan, whose Prime Minister Benazir Bhutto was overthrown by the military just before the Summit," said Gautam who discusses this in his memoir: *"Global Citizen from Gulmi: My Journey from the Hills of Nepal to the Halls of the United Nations."*

Meanwhile, Libyan leader Muammar Gaddafi, however, did make a visit to the UN in September 2009. In its report, the London Guardian said he "grabbed his 15 minutes of fame at the UN building in New York and ran with it. He ran with it so hard he stretched it to an hour and 40 minutes, six times longer than his allotted slot, to the dismay of UN organizers".

Gaddafi fully lived up to his reputation for eccentricity, bloody-mindedness and extreme verbiage, said the Guardian, as he tore up a copy of the UN charter in front of startled delegates, accused the Security Council of being an al-Qaida like terrorist body, called for George Bush and Tony Blair to be put on trial for the Iraq war, demanded $7.7 trillion in compensation for the ravages of colonialism on Africa, and wondered whether swine flu was a biological weapon created in a military laboratory.

Incidentally, according to one news report, there were 112 different spellings of the Libyan leader's name, both in English and Arabic, including Muammar el-Qaddafi, Muammar Gaddafi, Muammar al-Gathafi, Muammar El Kadhafi, Moammar el Kazzafi, Moamer, El Qathafi, Mu'Ammar, Gadafi, and Moamar Gaddafi, amongst others.

The Wall Street Journal ran a cartoon making fun of the

multiple spellings, with a visiting reporter, on a one-on-one interview in Tripoli, told the Libyan leader: "My editor sent me to find out whether you are Qaddafi, Khaddafi, Gadafi, Qathafi or Kadhafi?"

CHAPTER 10

UN outpost on the Gaza Strip Credit: UN Photo/JG

Give Us Your F-16 Fighter Planes & We will Give You Our Home-Made Bombs

The overwhelming Israeli firepower that continues to be unleashed on Palestinian militant groups in the longstanding battle in Gaza is perhaps reminiscent of the Algerian war of independence (1954-1962) when France, the colonial power, used its vastly superior military strength to strike back at the insurgents with brutal ferocity.

While France was accused of using its air force to napalm civilians in the countryside, the Algerians were accused of using handmade bombs hidden in women's handbags and left surreptitiously in cafes, restaurants and public places frequented by French nationals living in occupied territory.

In one of the memorable scenes in the 1967 cinematic classic "The Battle of Algiers," which re-created Algeria's war of independence against France, a handcuffed leader of the National Liberation Front (NLF), Ben M'Hidi, is brought before a group of highly partisan French journalists for interrogation.

One of the journalists asks M'Hidi: "Don't you think it is a bit cowardly to use women's handbags and baskets to carry explosive devices that kill so many innocent people [in cafes and night clubs?"

Responding with equal bluntness, the Algerian insurgent retorts: "And doesn't it seem to you even more cowardly to drop napalm bombs on unarmed villages on a thousand times more innocent victims?" "Of course, if we had your fighter planes, it would be a lot easier for us," he adds. "Give us your bombers, and you can have our handbags and baskets."

Like the Algerian insurgents, Palestinian militants were not fighting on a level battlefield – as the Israeli military unleashed its massive firepower on a virtually defenceless population in Gaza. On the looks of it, it was not a level battlefield but an uneven killing field.

"Perhaps it would be interesting to see the roles reversed: the Palestinians with American fighter planes and battle tanks and the Israelis with homemade rockets," says one Arab diplomat, striking a parallel with the Algerian insurgency.

Besides F-16 fighter planes, the Israelis also used a wide

array of U.S. weaponry, including Apache helicopters, M60 battle tanks, armored personnel carriers and heavy artillery. Israel's prodigious military strength and its economic stability were attributed largely to unlimited US assistance and political support from American politicians.

Pat Buchanan, a senior advisor to three US Presidents and twice candidate for the Republican presidential nomination, once infamously described the United States Congress as "Israeli-occupied territory" – apparently because of its unrelentingly blind support for the Jewish state.

When I walked out of a polling booth after voting in one of the US Senatorial elections in New York, I was accosted by a reporter and a cameraman for the Middle Eastern TV network AL Jazeera. The woman reporter, who was also a UN correspondent at that time, thrust the mike in front of me for my comments. I told her: "Frankly, I think US politicians are not running for office in the US House of Representatives or the Senate: they are running for a seat in the Israeli Knesset."

Meanwhile, an Arab diplomat recounts an Israeli cabinet meeting interrupted by an aide rushing in with the latest statistics on the state of the economy. The crops were down, growth was low, reserves were minimal, and inflation was high, he announced, portraying a rather gloomy economic picture.

Momentarily, the prime minister seemed flustered by the news – until he realized the aide was referring to the state of the Israeli economy. Breathing a sigh of relief, he joyfully exclaimed: "Thank God, for a moment I thought you were referring to the

American economy" – and went on with the business of the day, totally unfazed.

A longstanding story, doing the rounds at the United Nations, revealed the reality of Israeli life: its very existence has depended largely on the unrestrained political, economic, and military support of the United States. In November 2020, the US State Department put out an updated "Fact Sheet" detailing the strong political, economic, and military relationship between the US and Israel.

The United States is Israel's largest single trading partner. The U.S.-Israel Free Trade Agreement, signed in 1985, serves as the foundation for expanding trade and investment between our two countries. The U.S.-Israel economic and commercial relationship is anchored by bilateral trade of close to $50 billion in goods and services annually.

The Fact Sheet said Israel is home to more than 2,500 U.S. firms employing some 72,000 Israelis, while Israel is a top-15 foreign direct investor in the United States and supports an estimated 19,200 American jobs, according to the Department of Commerce.

The United States is committed to Israel's security and supporting its right to defend itself. "Under our 10-year Memorandum of Understanding, we provide $3.8 billion annually in security assistance to Israel".

In addition to financial support, the U.S and Israel maintain a high level of defense cooperation including joint military exercises, military research, and weapons development.

In 2020, President Trump brokered agreements to normalize relations between Israel and the United Arab Emirates, Bahrain, and Sudan – the first such agreements between Israel and Arab or Muslim-majority countries since 1994. The agreements between Israel and the UAE and Bahrain will also help advance the President's vision for finding a fair and lasting peace between Israel and the Palestinians.

In an interview back in 2009, Frida Berrigan, a senior research associate with the Arms Trade Resource Center at the World Policy Institute, pointed out that the bulk of Israel's current arsenal was composed of military equipment supplied under U.S. assistance programs.

Israel, she said, has been supplied with 226 F-16 fighter planes and attack jets, more than 700 M60 battle tanks, 6,000 armored personnel carriers and scores of transport planes, attack helicopters and utility and training aircraft, bombs, and tactical missiles of all kinds. In contrast, the hundreds of erratic rockets used by Hamas were so crude that most of them missed their targets.

"Israel has enormous military resources," said Dr. Natalie Goldring, a senior research fellow with the Center for Peace and Security Studies in the Edmund A. Walsh School of Foreign Service at Georgetown University. And recent events have demonstrated that Israel can destroy large areas of the Gaza Strip.

"But it cannot effectively defend its people against even relatively unsophisticated rockets launched from there,"

Goldring told IPS. Despite their size and sophistication, Israel's military forces have not produced peace. And they are not likely to do so. "There is no sign that either side will be successful in using force to convince the other to surrender," she added.

CHAPTER 11

*An interview with Prime Minister Mahathir Mohamad of Malaysia
at the UN's Indonesian Lounge*

The West is Really Looking for a Level Killing Field, not a Level Playing Field

When heads of government and foreign ministers make their annual pilgrimage to the United Nations in September, it is rare to hear hard-hitting, headline-grabbing political statements from the podium.

Malaysian Prime Minister Mahathir bin Mohamad, one of the world's most outspoken political leaders, was a newspaperman's dream – and a Western diplomat's nightmare.

Whenever he addressed the General Assembly or held a press conference at the UN, he was so outrageously candid that most journalists rarely missed his encounters or his verbal jousting.

The speeches before the General Assembly, and the UN press briefings that follow, are mostly dull and boringly monotonous. The exceptions, however, are rare.

When the UN celebrated its 50th anniversary in 1995, virtually every single head of state visiting New York for the General Assembly sessions decided to stay behind to participate in celebrations later that week.

But Mahathir, who was known to relentlessly accuse the big powers of manipulating the organization to their advantage, decided to skip the high-level event where world leaders were allocated five minutes to speak about the political virtues and the inglorious successes of the UN – even as the world body was mired in failures in three military hotspots at that time: Bosnia, Somalia, and Rwanda.

Asked why he was missing the much-ballyhooed event, Mahathir told reporters rather sarcastically: "In five minutes, you only have time to say how good things are. I am not good at saying how good things are when things are bad."

Mahathir, who called for the resignation of then-Secretary-General Kofi Annan for failing to assert himself during the crisis that led to the US invasion of Iraq, told the General Assembly that the UN's organs have been "cut out, dissected and reshaped so they may perform the way the puppet masters want."

"And this august institution in which we had pinned so

much hope, despite the safeguards supposed to be provided by the permanent five (UK, US, France, China, and Russia), this organization is today collapsing on its clay feet, helpless to protect the weak and the poor," he said back in 1995.

Mahathir, who at 94 made a political comeback as Prime Minister, May 2018-March 2020, said he was mindful of the "touching concern on the part of the West over human rights," but when the West manipulates economic sanctions causing millions of people to suffer, their rights are not considered human.

In one of his addresses to the General Assembly, Mahathir was his usual self: he criticized the manipulation of the UN by Western powers, ridiculed their concern over child labour, sympathized with Eastern European nations for having been taken for a glorious ride by the West and declared that globalization would eventually destroy markets.

Under globalization, the West is looking, not for a level playing field, but a level killing field, he said, as fragile Third World economies are in danger of being destroyed by open markets, currency de-controls and unfettered privatization.

One of the reasons why Malaysia has not been silenced is that it does not depend on economic handouts or military grants either from the US or the West, although Western investors and currency manipulators nearly destroyed the onetime booming economy.

Unlike Malaysia, most Third World nations that depend on Western generosity are usually silenced into submission on some of the most politically sensitive issues at the UN.

The Malaysian prime minister said the UN is often bypassed by the big and the powerful as new groupings of powerful nations or even one nation by itself seems to decide when to step in and when to step out.

When I interviewed him at the UN, he said: "While they like to wield power, they are inordinately unwilling to pay the price." Mahathir said that high-tech weapons are being deployed in so-called "pinpoint bombings" in order to avoid body bags from coming home. "The unwillingness to face the enemy often results in the unnecessary killing of innocent people and destruction of wrong targets," he noted.

Mahathir was specifically referring to the incessant bombing of Kosovo by NATO forces and the continued shelling of Iraq by the US and Britain at that time. Unfortunately, he said, no one should expect any change for as long as the UN belongs to the veto-wielding Big Five – the US, Britain, France, China, and Russia. The only saving grace, he said, are the UN agencies who do good humanitarian work in the field.

He pointed out that small countries lack a public forum to air their views. A longtime advocate of a global Third World newspaper, Mahathir accused the Western media of distorting everything that small countries say or do.

Still, he said, Third World nations are expected to give immunity to Western journalists. "They may break our laws, but no legal action may be taken against them. I would like to point out that in Malaysia, even the King and the hereditary

Sultans are not above the law," he told the General Assembly.

Mahathir said he was mindful of the "touching concern on the part of the West over human rights," but when the West manipulates economic sanctions causing millions of people to suffer, their rights are not considered human.

When the Malaysian economy was shattered by currency manipulators, it resulted in the deprivation of the right to work for millions of people. But Amnesty International had not uttered a single word about the violation of human rights, he said.

"What does the group say about the continuous bombing of Iraq where innocent people are being killed? Don't these people have the right to live?" he asked. "If you don't like their leader, you take action against the leader, but why do you starve the people?" he asked.

Mahathir also struck a note of sarcasm when he said that the West's concern over child labor and sweatshops is expressive of a sense of caring. Unfortunately, he argued, the concern is shown only when the products of child labor and sweatshops compete successfully with the products of highly paid, high-living, four-day week workers in industrial nations.

After a long traumatic experience, the Malaysian economy is now on the road to recovery. "With the blessings of Allah, we have now turned around," he added.

CHAPTER 12

Did Iraq's Notorious Abu Ghraib Prison Re-Open Under New Management?

When President Saddam Hussein ran one of the world's most authoritarian regimes in the militarily-volatile Middle East during 1979-2003, US newspapers routinely described him as "the strongman of Iraq" — as most journalists rightly view dictators worldwide.

But one of his political aides, described as "Saddam's right-hand man" (what if Saddam was left-handed?), took issue with a visiting US journalist when he rather hilariously challenged the description, "No, no, no", exclaimed the aide, unfamiliar with the nuances of the English language, "Saddam is no strong man. He is the strongest man in Iraq". The same response, which apparently came from one of the inhabitants in Saddam's birthplace, the city of Tikrit.

But Iraq's prodigious military strength was built on a massive arsenal of weapons, mostly from the then Soviet Union (under a 15-year Treaty of Friendship and Cooperation) and also from France and UK.

Still, the Saddam regime, which invaded neighboring Kuwait and temporarily occupied the country in 1990, was ousted from power after the US invasion of Iraq in March 2003. And the Bush administration justified the invasion, without the blessings of the UN Security Council, on the grounds that it was chasing Saddam's weapons of mass destruction (WMDs) – which never existed. The U.S. declared an end to the war on December 15, 2011, nearly eight years after invasion.

According to a joke circulating in Washington political circles, Saddam Hussein's notorious torture chamber in the Abu Ghraib prison in Baghdad – once held up as a symbol of barbarity – was never shut down. After the US occupation of the country, a signboard outside the prison chamber apparently read: "Under New Management."

The extent of the US administration's embarrassment following the publication of photos showing torture and abuse of Iraqi detainees in Abu Ghraib was evident in the fact that Washington postponed the release of the State Department's annual report on human rights abuses worldwide. The official reasons for the eleventh-hour postponement were not disclosed.

The report usually takes aim at virtually every country, most in the developing world, for human rights excesses while excluding US abuses from its pages. The question that was asked was: can Washington afford to take a holier-than-thou attitude when it beats up the rest of the world every year in its annual report?

Even the 'New York Times' admitted in its editorial that "the United States has been humiliated" to a point where government officials could not release the year's international human rights report "for fear of being scoffed at by the rest of the world."

"Internationally, there is little US credibility on human rights issues," said Phyllis Bennis of the Institute of Policy Studies in Washington. She attributed the lack of US credibility to two primary factors: "the blatantly political motives of human rights criticisms (largely ignoring abuses in US "client states" like Saudi Arabia and Egypt, and especially protecting Israel from the consequences of its human rights violations), and because of US denials in the past of its own human rights abuses."

The harrowing images of US soldiers brutalizing and humiliating Iraqi prisoners – aired worldwide triggered outrage not only in the Middle East but throughout the world. The photographs and television images included those of young Iraqis stripped naked and forced to pile up in a pyramid formation, while US soldiers grin at the hideous spectacle.

According to published reports, Iraqi detainees were also beaten up, tortured, threatened with rape and victimized by ferocious guard dogs. Dead bodies were later exhumed to ascertain the cause of death at the hands of soldiers or interrogators from the Central Intelligence Agency (CIA).

The United States, which actively participates in an annual ritual of "bashing" countries like Iran, Cuba, Syria, North Korea, Sudan and Myanmar at the U.N. Human Rights Commission, and later the successor Human Rights Council, in Geneva and at the General Assembly sessions in New York, had lost its moral authority to point an accusing finger at miscreants when it has problems in its own backyard, said diplomats from developing nations.

Meanwhile, in 1981, an Israeli attack by US-supplied F-15 and F-16 fighter planes destroyed the French-built Osirak nuclear reactor 18 miles south of Baghdad, described as the world's first airstrike against a nuclear plant. Following the attack, Iraq hosted an international conference, attended by world politicians, rebel leaders and journalists, in the Iraqi capital of Baghdad. The conference, needlessly to say, adopted a resolution vociferously condemning Israel for the attack.

After nearly a week-long stay, the contingent of journalists was promised an on-again, off-again press conference by Saddam Hussein keeping the reporters guessing. Along with some 10 or 15 international journalists, I was at a presidential palace to attend the briefing on the day of my departure. We were seated in what appeared to be an Assembly hall with most Arab journalists on the lower floor and the international journalists on the upper floor.

The press briefing that started around 6 pm went on and on late into the night past 10 pm. There were no English translations, and Arab journalists had the advantage over the rest of us. In characteristic Middle Eastern tradition, Saddam's responses went on for hours. A British journalist and I were expected to be at the airport for a midnight flight to Belgrade.

So, we both slipped out and told an Iraqi official of our plight. In our presence, he picked up the phone and spoke to someone in Arabic. After hanging up, he told us: "Don't worry, I just spoke to the head of Iraqi Airways and told him there are two journalists who should be on the midnight flight to Belgrade, but they are held up at a press conference with the President –and that flight should not leave until the two were on board".

And the aircraft remained on the tarmac until we got there long past midnight. Perhaps one of the advantages of being a guest flying in an airline-owned and operated by an authoritarian regime.

CHAPTER 13

Kofi Annan. Credit: UN Photo/Evan Schneider

When Kofi Annan Backed a Proposal to Ban Military Leaders Addressing the UN

The Secretary-General of the United Nations, who is a creature of member states, rarely challenges or defies his creators. But Kofi Annan did both. Surprisingly, he lived to tell the tale – but paid an unfairly heavy price after being hounded by the United States.

When the US invaded Iraq in March 2003, he described the invasion as "illegal" because it did not have the blessings of the 15-member UN Security Council, the only institution in the world body with the power to declare war and peace.

But the administration of President George W. Bush went after him for challenging its decision to unilaterally declare war against Iraq: an attack by a member state against another for no legally justifiable reason. The weapons of mass destruction (WMDs), reportedly in Iraq's military arsenal, which was one of the primary reasons for the invasion, were never found.

Subsequently, Annan came under heavy fire for misperceived lapses in the implementation of the "Oil-for-Food" program which was aimed at alleviating the sufferings of millions of Iraqis weighed down by UN sanctions.

Ian Williams, the author of 'UNtold: The Real Story of the United Nations in Peace and War', said, back in August 2018: «While I am heartened by the outpouring of appreciation for Kofi Annan, I can›t help but notice the contrast with the sound of silence when the Rupert Murdoch press and its followers had his back to the wall with the spurious Oil-for-Food crisis they had manufactured.» All too many stood back and stayed silent as Annan spent long months under constant sniper fire, he recounted.

While few now remember the Oil for Food crisis, said Williams, it was billed at the time as the "greatest financial scandal" in history. He said the so-called crisis "was a savage assault on Kofi's greatest asset – and his perceptible integrity took a severe personal toll, as people who should have known better kept their silence."

"It was, in fact, one of the greatest "fake news" concoctions in history, almost up there with Iraqi WMDs. That was no coincidence since many of the sources for both were the same," said Williams, a senior analyst who has written for newspapers and magazines around the world, including the Australian, The Independent, New York Observer, The Financial Times and The Guardian.

Annan was also the only Secretary-General who challenged the General Assembly for continuing to offer its podium to political leaders who come to power by undemocratic means or via military coups.

In 2004, when the Organization of African Unity (OAU), the predecessor to the present African Union (AU), barred coup leaders from participating in African summits, Annan singled it out as a future model to punish military dictators worldwide.

Annan went one step further and said he was hopeful that one day the General Assembly, the highest policy-making body in the Organization, would follow in the footsteps of the OAU and bar leaders of military governments from addressing the General Assembly. Annan's proposal was a historic first. But it never came to pass in an institution where member states, not the Secretary-General, rule the roost.

The outspoken Annan, a national of Ghana, also said that "billions of dollars of public funds continue to be stashed away by some African leaders – even while roads are crumbling, health systems are failing, school children have neither books nor desks nor teachers, and phones do not work." He also lashed out at African leaders who overthrow democratic regimes to grab power by military means.

Meanwhile, some of the military leaders who addressed the UN included Fidel Castro of Cuba, Col Muammar el-Qaddafi of Libya, Amadou Toure of Mali (who assumed power following a coup in 1991 but later served as a democratically elected President), and Jerry Rawlings of Ghana (who seized power in 1979, executed former heads of state but later served as a civilian president voted into power in democratic elections). As the International Herald Tribune reported, Rawlings was "Africa's first former military leader to allow the voters to choose his successor in a multi-party election."

In October 2020, the New York Times reported that at least 10 African civilian leaders refused to step down from power and instead changed their constitutions to serve a third or fourth term – or serve for life. These leaders included Presidents of Guinea (running for a third term), Cote d'Ivoire, Uganda, Benin, Burkina Faso, Central African Republic, Ghana, and Seychelles, among others. The only country where the incumbent was stepping down was Niger. Condemning all military coups, the Times quoted Umaro Sissoco Embalo, the president of Guinea-Bissau, as saying: "Third terms also count as coups."

And back in October 2006, the civilian government in Thailand was ousted when Prime Minister Thaksin Shinawatra was in New York to address the UN General Assembly sessions. Instead of returning home, where he was likely to face charges of corruption, Thaksin opted to fly to London, where he was in virtual political exile.

The bloodless military coup against a democratically elected government in Thailand forced the United States to review its military relations and suspend aid to one of Washington's long-standing political allies in Southeast Asia.

The administration of U.S. President George W. Bush, which was seeking UN sanctions against the military government in neighboring Myanmar (Burma), said the Thai military coup was a "U-turn" for democracy in that politically stable region.

Still, the best guarantee for survival – for visiting world leaders during the September UN General Assembly sessions – is to include all their military leaders, including the chiefs of the armed forces, the navy, and the air force, in the country's UN delegation so that they will be within sight at the General Assembly Hall – and not back home taking over the leadership of the country in military coups.

CHAPTER 14

Secretary-General Boutros Boutros-Ghali (second from left), responding to questions from correspondents outside the Security Council. On the left is Aly Teymour, Chief of Protocol, and on the right is Juan-Carlos Brandt, Associate Spokesman for the Secretary-General. Credit: UN Photo

UN Chiefs Who are Subservient to Ambassadors

The independence of the Secretary-General is a longstanding myth perpetuated mostly outside the United Nations. As an international civil servant, he is expected to shed his political loyalties when he takes office, and more importantly, never seek or receive instructions from any governments. But virtually every single Secretary-General—nine at last count – has played ball with the world's major powers in violation of Article 100 of the UN charter.

Perhaps those outside the UN assume the Secretary-General is all-powerful exercising unlimited powers. But in reality, he is only the chief administrative officer (CAO) who is subservient to presidents, prime ministers, foreign ministers and ambassadors accredited to the UN.

So, it was surprising when Antonio Guterres took office as Secretary-General back in 2017 when he was fully aware that despite his credentials as a former prime minister of Portugal (1995-2002) he had to be politically subservient even to UN ambassadors during his tenure in office beginning January 2017. Guterres was the first head of government to be elected UN chief.

A Nigerian ambassador once told a group of reporters of his encounter with one of his friends when he was in Africa to attend a conference. "I was in New York recently," his friend told the envoy ", and I met your boss". "My boss? Who is my boss", he asked? When he was told that his friend had met the Secretary-General, the Nigerian ambassador said: "He is not my boss. I am his boss."

When smoking was common in the UN corridors and committee rooms, the office of the Secretary-General sent a memo that specifically said "Smoking was Discouraged" in the UN building.

The Soviet Foreign Minister Sergey Lavrov, later the country's Foreign Minister, walked out of a Security Council meeting and began pulling out a cigarette in the presence of half a dozen reporters waiting for him outside the chamber. As he approached the reporters, one of them told him that the Secretary-General had banned smoking in the building.

And Lavrov shot back: "This building does not belong to the Secretary-General. It belongs to member states: he said, as he lit his cigarette. And he was right.

Dr Gamani Corea, Credit: United Nations

When Dr Gamani Corea, Secretary-General for the Geneva-based UN Conference on Trade and Development (UNCTAD) was holding court in the delegate's lounge, I asked him what he thought of the bitter dispute between then Secretary-General Boutros Boutros-Ghali and the United States over the Egyptian's determination to win re-election for a second term.

Dr. Corea pondered for a while and said he couldn't figure out why anyone in his right mind would ever want such a demanding job – and he was perhaps right. While holding the job himself, Trygve Lie of Norway, the first UN Secretary-General, once admitted it was "the most impossible job on this earth."

As a longtime UN watcher said: "If you don't play ball with the P-5 – or cozy up to them – you'd never get the job". And as someone once rightly pointed out, the Secretary-General really plays a subservient role of a mere "Secretary" to the big powers doing their bidding but asserts his authority as a commanding

"General" to the rest of the member states. Perhaps that justifies the title of "Secretary-General," two titles rolled into one.

And every Secretary-General has to win the goodwill of the P-5 to get another five-year extension on the job. But a proposal to make him more independent with a single, seven-year term in office never got off the ground.

A 1996 study sponsored by two major think tanks implicitly accused some of the world's big powers of manipulating the election of the Secretary-General so as to ensure that U.N. heads are political creatures with no minds of their own.

"It is impossible to escape the impression, that many governments, including some of the most powerful, do not want a strong, independent leader as Secretary-General," said the study published under the auspices of the New York-based Ford Foundation and the Dag Hammarskjold Foundation of Sweden.

The authors of the study – Brian Urquhart and Erskine Childers, both senior UN officials – said the selection of the Secretary-General is quite literally part of "an old-boy network." "The United Nations is an intergovernmental organization, and governments have no intentions of giving up control of it."

Boutros Boutros-Ghali of Egypt, the only Secretary-General to be denied a second term because of a negative US veto, bared the insidious political maneuvering that goes inside the glasshouse.

Boutros-Ghali also recounted how Secretary of State Warren Christopher had tried to convince him to publicly declare that he will not run for a second term as secretary-General. But he refused. "Surely, you cannot dismiss the Secretary-General of the United Nations by a unilateral diktat of the United States. What about the rights of the other (14) Security Council members?", he asked Christopher. But Christopher "mumbled something inaudible and hung up, deeply displeased".

Boutros-Ghali also said that in late 1996, US Ambassador to the UN Madeleine Albright, on instructions from the US State Department, was fixated on a single issue that had dominated her life for months: the "elimination" of Boutros-Ghali.

Under-Secretary-General Joseph Verner Reed, an American, is quoted as saying that he had heard Albright say: "I will make Boutros think I am his friend; then I will break his legs." After meticulously observing her, Boutros-Ghali concludes that Albright had accomplished her diplomatic mission with skill.

"She had carried out her campaign with determination, letting pass no opportunity to demolish my authority and tarnish my image, all the while showing a serene face, wearing a friendly smile, and repeating expressions of friendship and admiration," he writes. "I recalled what a Hindu scholar once said to me: there is no difference between diplomacy and deception".

CHAPTER 15

Credit: United Nations

A Battle of Political Wits in the Security Council

During the height of the Cold War between the United States and the Soviet Union, and particularly in the 1960s, the United Nations was the ideological battle ground where the Americans and the Soviets pummeled each other – metaphorically speaking — either on the floor of the cavernous General Assembly hall or at the horse-shoe table of the Security Council.

Perhaps one of the most memorable war of words took place in October 1962 when the politically-feisty US Ambassador Adlai Stevenson challenged Soviet envoy Valerian Zorin over allegations that the USSR, perhaps under cover of darkness, had moved nuclear missiles into Cuba—and within annihilating distance of the United States.

Speaking at a tense Security Council meeting, Stevenson admonished Zorin: "I remind you that you didn't deny the existence of these weapons. Instead, we heard that they had suddenly become defensive weapons. But today — again, if I heard you correctly — you now say they don't exist, or that we haven't proved they exist, with another fine flood of rhetorical scorn."

"All right sir", said Stevenson, "let me ask you one simple question. Do you, Ambassador Zorin, deny that the USSR has placed and is placing medium and intermediate-range missiles and sites in Cuba?" "Yes or no? Don't wait for the translation: yes or no?", Stevenson insisted with a tone of implied arrogance.

Speaking in Russian through a UN translator (who faithfully translated the US envoy's sentiments into English), Zorin shot back: "I am not in an American courtroom, sir, and therefore I do not wish to answer a question that is put to me in the fashion in which a prosecutor does. In due course, sir, you will have your reply. Do not worry."

Not to be outwitted, Stevenson howled back: "You are in the court of world opinion right now, and you can answer yes or no. You have denied that they exist. I want to know if …I've understood you correctly." When Zorin said he will provide the answer in "due course", Stevenson famously declared: "I am prepared to wait for my answer until hell freezes over."

The debates and resolutions in the Security Council

are mostly on the maintenance of international peace and security. But it also had its moments of levity. Ambassador Jamil Baroody, the longstanding Saudi envoy to the UN (1945-79) and described as the dean of the UN diplomatic corps, was a "colorful maverick" known for his mile-long speeches. In its obituary, the New York Times described him as a UN "landmark" who was known for his shouting matches – while holding the distinction of making one of the longest speeches in the history of the world body.

So, whenever he held forth at Council meetings, the US ambassador was known to slip out of the chamber and return at the tail end of his speeches. When Baroody once noticed the American envoy returning to his seat, he turned to the President of the Security Council and said: "Mr President, I noticed the honorable US representative was not in the chamber when I spoke. So, I am going to read my statement all over again for his benefit". The US envoy remained trapped in the chamber.

For long now, there have been four strong contenders for permanent seats in the UN Security Council (UNSC) – Germany, India, Japan and Brazil— with Africa insisting on two permanent seats with vetoes. But during a discussion on reforms in the Security Council in 2019, one delegate made a strong case for a permanent seat for the 57-member Organization of Islamic Cooperation (OIC), the largest single coalition of Muslim countries at the UN.

Perhaps, in a slip of the tongue, he urged member states to ensure permanent membership to the "Islamic State" – which is really one of the extremist organizations operating out of the Middle East. The Islamic State of Iraq and the Levant (ISIL), also known as the Islamic State of Iraq and Syria (ISIS) is officially known as the Islamic State (IS). And ISIS as a permanent member of the UNSC?

Meanwhile whenever the General Assembly or the Security Council holds a meeting, the speeches of the delegates are routinely distributed no sooner the speaker begins his address. These speeches marked "check against delivery", are left on the desks of all member states, 15 in the Security Council and 193 in the General Assembly.

So, there was a moment of hilarity when the Indian Foreign Minister picked up, not his speech, but a speech made by an earlier speaker and began reading it. Iftikhar Ali, the UN correspondent for the Association Press of Pakistan (APP), who covered that meeting, told me it was a monumental faux pas by the Indian External Affairs Minister when he read out the Portuguese delegate's speech, instead of India's, before an aide intervened and he turned to his own text.

During the debate on security and development, a subject on which most delegates made identical speeches, he mistakenly read the wrong speech for about three minutes before India's envoy pointed to the Indian speech in a stack of papers in front of his minister. With mikes on, an embarrassed foreign minister whispered to his ambassador: Should I read it from the beginning? The ambassador said, "Yes, you can start again".

The Indian minister read Portuguese foreign minister Luis

Amado's speech, without realizing his mistake, as the first portion was about development and security, the theme of the Council's debate. As the minister continued, Ali said a couple of lines was definitely out of sync: "On a more personal note, allow me to express my profound satisfaction regarding the happy coincidence of having two members of the Portuguese Speaking Countries (CPLP), Brazil and Portugal, together here today," the minister said.

He also went on to say, "The European Union is also responding in this manner in coordination with the United Nations..." At this point, the Indian envoy intervened and told him to restart. The Portuguese minister had already delivered his statement before India.

CHAPTER 16

An Indian Ocean Island Comes with an Expiry Date

Just after a band of mercenaries tried to oust the government of the Maldives, I asked a Maldivian diplomat about the strength of his country's standing army. "Standing army?", the diplomat asked with mock surprise, "We don't even have a sitting army."

With a population of about 250,000, back in March 1999, the Maldives was perhaps one of the few countries with no fighter planes, combat helicopters, warships, missiles, or battle tanks. As a result, the island's fragile defenses attracted a rash of free-lance mercenaries and bounty hunters who tried to take over the country twice – once in 1979, and a second time in 1988.

Although both attempts failed, the Maldives refused to drop its defenses. It not only initiated a proposal seeking a UN security umbrella to protect the world's militarily vulnerable mini states but also backed a still-evolving international convention to outlaw mercenaries.

Categorized by the UN as a small island developing state (SIDS), and with a current population of over 540,000, the Maldives has for long been threatened with rising sea level and in danger of being wiped off the face of the earth. A growing number of SIDS, including Papua New Guinea, Samoa, Tonga, Nauru and Kiribati, have made a strong case for a stand-alone goal for the protection of oceans in the post-2015 development agenda known as the SDGs.

In April 2010, the World Bank described the Maldives as a low-lying archipelago with more territorial sea than land while being exposed to the risks of intensifying weather events. Sea level rise represents an existential threat to the country. With future sea levels projected to increase in the range of 10 to 100 centimeters by the year 2100, the entire country could be submerged.

Besides tourism, one of the biggest foreign exchange earners for the Maldives was canned tuna fish comprising about 65.9% of total exports. Fathulla Jameel, the Permanent Representative of the Maldives to the UN and later the country's Foreign Minister, was gifted with a sense of humor. Asked about the threat of sea level rise, he told me: "Our country is like our can of tuna fish. It comes with an expiry date."

Fluent in Arabic, he strengthened his relationship with Middle Eastern countries and was frequently seen in the company of Arab diplomats in the UN delegate's lounge. Fathulla was known to regale his friends with anecdotes he had picked up during his visits to Arab capitals.

Perhaps one of his most enduring jokes related to the eccentric Libyan leader Muammar el-Qaddafi who made several unsuccessful attempts to form a single Federation of Arab Republics (FAR) seeking to merge with Egypt and Syria in order to create a unified Arab republic, with the possibility of some of the North African countries like Morocco and Algeria joining the federation later. But the plans never got off the ground.

So, when Qaddafi visited China in 1982, he met with Chinese leader Deng Xiaoping and offered a proposal to merge Libya with China in a sprawling Asian-Arab Federation. The Chinese leader, who was presiding over a country with over 1.0 billion people, apparently pondered for a while, so the joke goes, and asked Qaddafi how big his country's population was. Told it was a paltry 3.4 million, Deng told Qaddafi: "Why don't you bring them along when you next visit China?"

During the 1970s, I had a close working relationship with Maldivian diplomats and occasionally occupied one of their seats at the General Assembly hall (and those were the days when anyone with a UN pass could walk into the hall without the scrutiny of security officers). And some of my Sri Lankan friends at the UN thought I was moonlighting as a Maldivian diplomat.

In the 1970s, the Maldivian Ambassador was Ahmed Zaki, a former Prime Minister who spent time as a political prisoner in an uninhabited island (at the last count, the Maldives comprised over 1,200 islands scattered across the Indian Ocean). When the government changed in the capital of Male, he made a political comeback: emerging from a lonely prisoner living in isolation --to a resident of New York City in the company of more than 7.9 million inhabitants. The Hongkong based regional magazine Asiaweek ran the story under the headline: "The Pit and the Pendulum".

Unlike most diplomats I knew, Zaki was a breed apart and willingly participated in some of New York's city's rituals in the 1970s. I once took him to a pot party – illegal under the law— at a friend's residence in the Upper West Side of Manhattan. When we arrived at the apartment, we found about ten young "potheads", both men and women, seated on the carpeted floor and "passing the joint". I introduced the ambassador and jokingly announced: "Hey guys. Don't worry about a Police raid because we are covered by diplomatic immunity." A false assurance.

But we continued smoking pot till late into the night. To me, it was a novel experience because I had never touched liquor, cigarettes nor cigars (even when I visited Cuba twice, a country which produced Fidel Castro and the world's best cigars, I was told). Incidentally, in December 2020, the US House of Representatives passed sweeping legislation decriminalizing marijuana at the federal level and expunging non-violent marijuana-related convictions.

I once accompanied Zaki to an electronics store for the purchase of a TV set. When he produced his tax-free card (which all diplomats are privileged to carry entitling them to both duty free and tax-free purchases), the store clerk looked at it and said: "Where the hell is the Mald-i-ves?" and added: "I think you guys create these countries just to make tax free purchases.".

Meanwhile, when a delegation from the capital, mostly young diplomats, arrived in New York for the General Assembly sessions, Zaki apparently told the delegates, perhaps half-seriously: "When you are here for the UN sessions, there are only two things you should know: Where the UN is located – and who Mr. Deen is?"

When I gleefully mentioned this to Foreign Minister Fathulla Jameel, he provided the punchline: "And the Ambassador added: Because I want to you avoid him."

CHAPTER 17

Mario Lubetkin (left), Director General of IPS News Agency, presents Secretary-General Kofi Annan with the Inter Press Service International Achievement Award 2006, for his lasting contributions to peace, security, development, gender empowerment and human rights, at the annual IPS award ceremony, at the UN Headquarters in New York in December 2006

A News Agency that Leads but Doesn't Bleed

When Kofi Annan leaves the United Nations, after an eventful 10-year tenure as secretary-general, there will be one prized possession he said he will virtually hand-carry: The Inter Press Service (IPS) International Achievement Award 2006. "After ten exhilarating years as secretary-general, it is humbling to be recognized for doing what you love to do," he told a gathering of nearly 300 U.N. staffers, ambassadors, and representatives of non-governmental organizations (NGOs) at the annual IPS award ceremony held at the U.N. delegate's dining room.

When the United Nations launched a new series in 2004

drawing attention to the "10 Most Under-Reported Stories of the Year", IPS was far ahead of the curve having covered at least seven of the ten stories in a single year: AIDS orphans in Africa; Women as Peacemakers; the Hidden World of the Stateless; Policing for Peace; the Girl Soldier; Indigenous Peoples and a Treaty for the Disabled.

Shashi Tharoor, a former U.N. under-secretary-general and head of the Department of Public Information (DPI), who originated the series, recounted the role of IPS in covering under-reported stories.

Reiterating his comments, Tharoor paid a tribute to IPS during its 50th-anniversary celebrations in August 2014: "I have followed IPS' reporting for three decades and worked with them at close quarters during my media-related assignments at the United Nations.

"I found IPS an excellent source of news and insight about the developing world, covering stories the world's dominant media outlets too often ignore," said Tharoor, later a member of parliament for Thiruvananthapuram in India's Lok Sabha. He said IPS reporters marry the highest professional standards of journalism to an institutional commitment to covering stories of particular concern to the global South.

"They are indispensable to any reader who wishes to stay abreast of what's happening in developing countries around the world," said Tharoor, a prolific writer and author of several books.

IPS was set up in 1964, the same year as the Group of 77

(G77) and the U.N. Conference on Trade and Development (UNCTAD). The news agency was a brainchild of two journalists: Roberto Savio and Pablo Piancentini. But in its news coverage over the last 57 years, IPS has led mostly with "unsexy" and "un-bleeding" stories, long ignored by the mainstream media.

Judged by its peers, IPS reporters were honored three times for excellence in UN reporting during the annual awards ceremony by the UN Correspondents' Association (UNCA). We began with a "honorable mention", then went on to win a Bronze medal, (shared with the Washington Post), and two gold medals, the second one shared with Reuters, in two consecutive years: 2012 and 2013.

As IPS commemorated its 50th anniversary, its news coverage of the developing world and the United Nations was singled out for praise because of its primary focus on social and politico-economic issues on the U.N. agenda, including poverty, hunger, population, children, gender empowerment, education, health, refugees, human rights, disarmament, the global environment, and sustainable development.

IPS news agency, which has relentlessly covered the developing world, has suffered both under repressive authoritative regimes and in war-ravaged countries where our journalists have either been detained, tortured or beaten to death in the line of duty in Asia, Africa, the Middle East and Latin America.

But for most surviving families, the tragedy has been

doubly devastating because the killer or killers have never been apprehended, prosecuted, or convicted in any court of law in their respective home countries—or in some cases, their bodies never recovered.

The most glaring example was the fate of 30-year-old Richard de Zoysa, the IPS Bureau Chief in Sri Lanka, who was abducted, tortured, killed and dropped from a helicopter into the ocean – a crime reportedly perpetrated by "death squads". His bloated body was washed ashore in the Sri Lankan capital Colombo's, suburbs. The horrendous politically motivated crime, which took place in February 1990, is still one of the unresolved murders after 31 long years.

In 2006, Alla Hassan, the IPS correspondent in Iraq, was shot and killed while driving to work in a war zone where killings were routine with little or no rule of law. And in Argentina in the mid-1970s, two IPS journalists, Luis Guagnini and Roberto Carri were both abducted at the end of their working day in the IPS Bureau in Buenos Aires – and their dead bodies were never recovered.

In a February 2013 piece titled "Censorship by Murder Will Not Silence Truth", IPS Regional Editor for Asia Kanya d'Almeida wrote that even though Sri Lanka experienced a "reign of terror" battling two insurgencies in the South and the North in the 1990s, "no one expected that one of its victims would be Richard de Zoysa." She described him as "the progeny of two powerful Colombo families, star of the English-language stage, a well-known newscaster and bureau chief of the Rome-based Inter Press Service (IPS) news agency, whose dispatches on Sri Lanka throughout the 1980s earned him a reputation at home and abroad as an exceptionally prolific writer."

Meanwhile, at a formal ceremony attended by diplomats, senior U.N. officials and journalists, the United Nations presented its 2008 'South-South Leadership Award' to IPS for its role in promoting stronger ties among developing nations and media outlets.

'We consider ourselves privileged to accept this award – and we also view this as a recognition of the work we have been doing to highlight South-South cooperation in the field of communications during the last 45 years,' said IPS Director-General Mario Lubetkin in a ceremony at the UN in December 2008. 'As a news agency of the global South, IPS follows the U.N. development agenda very closely,' he added.

The award was presented by the Special Unit for South-South Cooperation within the U.N. Development Program (UNDP), which has honored individuals and institutions over the last four years.

Lubetkin said the main thrust of IPS news reporting has been – and continues to be – on issues long neglected by the mainstream media. These include hunger, poverty alleviation, population, children, HIV/AIDS, gender empowerment and the environment, just to name a few.

The Washington-based Population Institute, which gave its annual media awards for development reporting, singled out IPS as "the most conscientious news service" for coverage relating to population and development. IPS won the award nine times in the 1990s, beating out the major wire services year in and year out, occasionally conceding to Reuters and the Associated Press (AP).

Congratulating IPS on its 50th anniversary in 2014, U.N. Secretary-General Ban Ki-moon was quick to applaud IPS' "relentless focus on issues of concern to the developing world – from high-level negotiations on economic development to on-the-ground projects that improve health and sanitation. "I thank IPS for raising global public awareness about matters at the heart of the U.N.'s agenda, and I hope it will have an even greater impact in the future," he added.

In its advocacy role, IPS was in the forefront of a longstanding campaign, led by world leaders, activists and women's groups, for the creation of a separate U.N. entity to reinforce equal rights for women and gender empowerment.

CHAPTER 18

ON AND OFF THE BEATEN TRACK...

From the Sublime to the Hilarious

An Untouchable at a New York Strip Club

A New York newspaper once ran a story of how a visiting head of state, along with his entourage, took time off to visit a strip club in Manhattan featuring lap dancers. When one of the strippers got temptingly close to the head of state offering him a sensuous lap dance, one of his burly security officers, jumped into the middle of the act, shouting: "Don't touch the Prime Minister." Mercifully, the Prime Minister was not a so-called "untouchable."—now called Dalits, a description applicable to one of the lower castes Hindus in India.

Mistaken Identity

Madeleine Albright, a former US envoy to the UN and the first female US Secretary of State (1997-2001), once recounted with relish an incident that reportedly took place at the Heathrow airport when she was running late for a meeting in London. She asked one of the Immigration officers: "Do you who I am? "No", snickered the officer "But we have doctors here who can help you figure that out".

Kleptocracy, Anyone?

The late Mobutu Sese Seko, president of former Zaire (now the Democratic Republic of the Congo), was singled out as one of "the world's most corrupt leaders". Asked at a press conference whether he was the second wealthiest political leader in the world, a seemingly outraged Mobutu shouted back: "It's a lie. It's a lie," and then added with a straight face, "I am only the fourth richest." Meanwhile, an October 1991 report in the Washington Post quoted Mobutu as saying: "If you want to steal, steal a little cleverly, in a nice way. Only if you steal so much as to become rich overnight, you will be caught."

The Vanishing Act

At the height of the Cold War back in the 1960s, a Peruvian diplomat, Dr. Victor Andres Belaunde, characterized the United Nations as a politically wobbly institution that survives only at the will – and pleasure – of the five big powers. Simplifying his argument in more realistic terms, he said: "When two small powers have a dispute, the dispute disappears. When a great power and a small power are in conflict, the small power disappears. And when two great powers have a dispute, the United Nations disappears." And more appropriately, it is the UN Security Council (UNSC) that vanishes into oblivion, particularly when big powers clash, warranting a ceasefire, not in some distant military conflict, but inside the UNSC chamber itself.

Mata Hari's at the UN?

The best way to figure out the nationality of a diplomat, according to a longstanding anecdote, is to watch how he responds when he is introduced to a newly arrived woman diplomat at a reception or a cocktail party. The Englishman would be very formal, ask what committee she was covering and what her previous assignments were. The Frenchman would bow, reach for her upturned palm, and gracefully plant a kiss. The American, after five minutes of flirting, would ask her for a "dinner date." The Russian would rush back to his office and telex the foreign ministry for instructions—while checking whether she is a spy.

Republic of China & USSR Still Hold Sway

The Republic of China (Taiwan) withdrew from the United Nations when it was ousted from its highly prized permanent seat in the UN Security Council (UNSC) about 50 years ago. But according to the UN charter, it still remains one of the five permanent members of the most powerful body in the Organization—perhaps much to the delight of the Taiwanese.

The resolution that was adopted by the UN General Assembly (UNGA) back in October 1971 declared the People's Republic of China (PRC) as the legitimate representative of mainland China paving the way for the immediate takeover of the seat from ROC. Although the Charter has been amended about five times—described as a laborious process requiring a two-thirds majority in the 193-member General Assembly— there have been no serious attempts to rectify the UNSC anomaly.

And a second shortcoming in the UN charter is the continued listing of the Union of Soviet Socialist Republics (USSR) as a permanent member of the Security Council, when it ceased to exist back in 1991, with the Russian Federation assuming the rights and obligations as a successor state. Currently, the five permanent members (P5s) of the UNSC are the US, France, PRC, UK and the Russian Federation. But the Charter, which looks like a relic of a bygone era, begs to differ.

Meanwhile, there is old saying that If you want to do business in China, don't talk about the three "T"s, – Tibet, Taiwan and Tiananmen Square.

Rigged Elections

A head of state, who presided over an authoritarian, despotic regime in Southeast Asia, was once asked about rigged elections in his country. "I promised I will give you the right to vote," he said, "But I did not say anything about counting those votes."

A New Form of Torture

When North Koreans, who usually lead frugal lives and are mostly starved of consumer goods, are caught trying to infiltrate South Korea as spies, they are reportedly subjected to new form of torture. The South Koreans, according to a widespread rumor, march the infiltrators through Seoul supermarkets overflowing with groceries and consumer goods—a sight never seen in the North. That say the South Koreans is absolute torture for the North Koreans.

Fake News

During an interview with a journalist, a deputy Prime Minister of a Southeast Asian country, was asked about the leading newspapers in his country. "We don't have any leading newspapers," he said, "because all our newspapers are misleading."

The UN as Censor

When the UN commemorated its 50th anniversary in 1995, an internationally renowned journalist Jonathan Power, syndicated columnist, and former foreign affairs columnist for the International Herald Tribune, was contracted to edit and publish a book titled "A Vision of Hope". The contributors included Maurice Strong, a former Secretary-General of the 1992 UN Conference on the Environment and Development (UNCED) and Mahbub ul Haq, editor of the UNDP's widely acclaimed annual Human Development Report.

But just before the commemorative issue went into print, the UN made some 70 drastic cuts throughout the text, including all references to human rights violations by member states. Instructions were given to replace certain photographs and change numerous photo captions—largely deleting country references. Eventually, following lengthy negotiations overdraft texts, a compromise was reached whereby the names of the authors were withdrawn from all articles, according to Power. The same institution that framed the Universal Declaration of Human Rights stood accused of suppressing information about human rights abuses and became a censor in its own right. Presiding over these cuts were Secretary-General Boutros Boutros-Ghali (1992-1996) and Gillian Martin Sorensen, Special Advisor to the Secretary-General for Public Policy.

A Future President at the Battle of Algiers

One of my all-time favorite movies is the 1966 award-winning " Battle of Algiers" by the Italian Director Gillo Pontecorvo – how the Algerians fought a brutal war of independence against the French. After watching the movie in the mid-1970s, I was stepping out of the theater – the Carnegie Hall Cinema in mid-town Manhattan – when I saw the Foreign Minister of Algeria and his wife waiting in line for the 10 pm movie: Abdelaziz Bouteflika, later President of Algeria (1999-2019). It was one of those "only in New York" stories. A future head of state waiting in line outside a New York movie theater on a Saturday night. It could have been straight out of a Woody Allen movie.

A Cash-Starved City

I was reporting from the Swedish capital of Stockholm for 12 consecutive years, firstly covering the annual international conferences on water – on the invitation of the Stockholm International Water Institute (SIWI) – and later the annual conferences on peace and development, on the invitation of the Stockholm International Peace Research Institute (SIPRI). By 2019, I found two new developments in a City I treated as my second home. There was hardly a store, a restaurant or a supermarket which accepted hard cash. All signs outside stores read: "No Cash. Cards Only." And I found most Swedes were paying with their smartphones, a step ahead of credit cards. As a result, a bank manager was quoted in the New York Times as saying: "We don't have any bank robberies in Sweden now because our banks don't have any cash."

As I walked the streets of Stockholm – while also visiting neighboring towns which were only a train ride away – I noticed an increasing number of women in hijabs and men wearing beards. They were mostly refugees and asylum seekers from war-ravaged Afghanistan, Syria, Yemen and politically troubled Iraq. Traditionally, most Swedes had last names such as Eriksson, Johansson, Karlsson, Andersson, Larsson and Svensson, indicating either a son of Erik, a son of Karl or a son of Johan. The new arrivals, who were mostly Muslims, have been following this tradition and naming their sons either Mohamedson or Ahamedson. An example of cultural integration? Perhaps.

An Eskimo in the UN Neighborhood?
The IPS office on the UN's fourth floor was an occasional meeting place for representatives of liberation movements accredited to the UN, including the PLO and FRETILIN. One regular visitor was Jose Ramos-Horta, designated as foreign minister in the government-in-exile set up by the liberation movement FRETILIN (Revolutionary Front for an Independent East Timor). Winner of the 1996 Nobel Peace Prize and later president of East Timor (2007-2012), Ramos-Horta, according to a widely circulated anecdote, was at a dinner in a restaurant frequented by delegates, in the UN neighborhood, where waiters politely asked guests from what country they were from.

When asked, he proudly claimed he was from East Timor, (a former Portuguese possession that was under Indonesian control from 1975 to 1999). "So, you are an Eskimo?", said the waiter displaying his geographical ignorance. "'No, no, no," replied Ramos-Horta: "I am not an Eskimo, I am from country called East Timor." After he completed his presidency in 2012, he was appointed as the United Nations' Special Representative and Head of the United Nations Integrated Peacebuilding Office in Guinea-Bissau (UNIOGBIS) in January 2013. When I met him outside the UN on First Avenue, I double-checked the anecdote –- and he confirmed it did happen. And laughed.

Ambassador for Life

In terms of diplomatic protocol, the title of ambassador is virtually for life. So, when I met a former PRUN, holding a ministerial portfolio in his post-ambassadorial life back in his home country, I continued to address him as "Ambassador," as protocol demands, during a brief encounter in the UN delegate's lounge- – and added, "once an Ambassador always an Ambassador." And he was quick to respond with a laugh: "Yes, once a prostitute, always a prostitute."

Reds Under the Beds?

In class, one of the professors at Columbia University was explaining the red-baiting that went on during the late 1940s, and 50's when Wisconsin Senator Joseph McCarthy, in his crusade against Communism, led a series of investigations and hearings to reveal – imaginary or real—Communist infiltration into the US government. There was hysterical paranoia about "reds" and "Communists" in the deep state. The extent of McCarthyism was evident, he said when there were two groups of demonstrators – the pro Communists and the anti-Communists—staging protests and counter-protests in Times Square. When the demonstrations got unruly, the cops dragged some of the protestors from the streets, and bodily threw them into Police paddy wagons when one of them pleaded: "I am anti-Communist. I am anti-Communist". The cop shouted back: "I don't care what goddam brand of Communist you are". Talk of Communist Paranoia?

How do you Steal an F-1 Mirage Fighter Plane?

What is the magnitude of a robbery when the goods stolen include fighter planes, combat helicopters, surface-to-air missiles and over 5,000 pieces of artillery? The loot was monumental, said the Kuwaitis, who accused Iraq of stripping the country's military arsenal of some of the world's most sophisticated weapons purchased with oil money. The weapons – including eight F-1 Mirage fighter planes, 245 armored personnel carriers, 3,750 anti-tank missiles and six battle tanks – were apparently carted away by the Iraqis when they invaded Kuwait in August 1990. The Kuwaitis eventually gave an ultimatum to Iraq: either return all of the stolen property or there will no end to UN sanctions. Although Iraq returned "a substantial quantity of Kuwaiti property," there were many items still in Iraqi possession and which Iraq said, "is under obligation to return to Kuwait."

When BBG Defied the US

When Secretary-General Boutros Boutros-Ghali (1992-96) ran for a second term in office, he defied the veto-wielding United States and eventually lost his bid for re-election – although 14 of the 15 members of the Security Council overwhelmingly voted for him. The one US veto destroyed his chances of re-election. Unfortunately, his re-election campaign also coincided with the US presidential elections of 1996, and for a moment, he became an object of undeserved ridicule. Patrick Buchanan, a right-wing Republican, and presidential aspirant kept mocking at Boutros-Ghali calling him by a nickname: "Boo-Boo Ghali". Expressing fears that American troops may one day come under UN command, Buchanan said: "We don't take orders from Boo-Boo Ghali."

Eastern Europe? Still Alive -- and Running for Office?

Since the collapse of the Soviet Union back in 1991, Eastern Europe as a political and geographical entity gradually ceased to exist – except at the United Nations, where it is still alive and running for office. The countries of the former Eastern Europe, which range from Bulgaria and Georgia to Slovenia and Ukraine, have been virtually absorbed either by the revamped European Union (EU) or the North Atlantic Treaty Organization (NATO). All electoral positions in the United Nations traditionally rotates among the five regional groups: the Asia-Pacific States (55 members), the African States (54), the Eastern European States (23), the Latin American and Caribbean States (33) and the Western European and Other States (29).

As one UN diplomat told me back in December 2020: Montenegro is a member of NATO, has recognized Kosovo and is in the final chapter of its negotiations with the EU and may be the first country to enter the EU once the process is complete. "I think it's ahead of North Macedonia and Albania. So, one may wonder what its foreign policy has to do with Eastern Europe -- as it may seem at odds with many of them!" But many diplomats argue there is no reason for an Eastern European regional group to exist at the United Nations. "They are now an appendage of Western Europe," said an Asian diplomat. "They exist at the U.N. purely to seek electoral posts."

The Gang That Couldn't Shoot Straight

The late Marco Napoli, one of the stalwarts of the IPS UN bureau, began his early professional career as both a New York and UN correspondent for several international news organizations, including the Italian Il Progresso News, back in the 1960s, long before he became Regional Director, IPS North America.

As part of his beat, he had to cover some of the shenanigans of reputed Mafia families in New York, relying largely on anonymous sources in New York City Police Department's (NYPD) Organized Crime Control Bureau. Marco once recounted one of his more memorable experiences interviewing a legendary Mafia boss in the backseat of a limousine in New York's famed Central Park.

Fearful of any possible attacks on the head honcho, who was apparently on a hit list, Marco was uneasily looking over his shoulder as he continued with his interview. Sensing Marco's nervousness, the Mafia boss looked at him, tapped at the tinted car window with his clenched fist, and told Marco: "Don't worry, it's bullet proof."

The Last Supper

Speaking of the Mafia, some of the most legendary killings took place in New York city restaurants, including the Umberto Clam House, Rao's, Nuova Villa Tammaro and Sparks Steak House (as listed in the National Crime Syndicate website). And in what was described as one of the most iconic scenes in movie history, Michael Corleone, played by Al Pacino, kills a Mafia boss and a corrupt police captain in Louie's Restaurant in the Bronx, as depicted in the 1972 Academy Award-winning Hollywood classic "The Godfather",

So, when an Italian reporter in the UN press corps was invited to dinner by a Mafia chieftain at a Brooklyn restaurant, he was rather reluctant to accept the invitation because, according to a joke circulating at the time, the maître d' at this restaurant usually asks the guest: "Sir, you want the shooting section or the non-shooting section" Obviously, the shooting section in New York's Italian restaurants is more hazardous to your health than the smoking section.

Inter Press or Intern Press Service?

During summer months, we had nearly a dozen students as interns working out of our office, with the overflow in the bullpen area on the fourth floor. One of our interns scanned our letter head and renamed our news agency: INTER PRESS SERVICE was transformed into INTER(N) PRESS SERVICE. Perhaps rightly so, particularly in the summer.

Among other guidelines, our interns were advised never to use cliches in their stories – but rather update or give a new twist to old clichés. Snail's pace? Slow as a tortoise? A resounding No. The UN's bloated bureaucracy, I once wrote, is known to move at the combined pace of a paralytic snail and a limping tortoise. "Born with a silver spoon in the mouth?" No. That's another cliché.

At the 1988 Democratic Convention, Ann Richards, a former Governor of Texas, took a well-aimed potshot at the Republican nominee George W. Bush, later President, describing him as someone who was "born with a silver foot in his mouth". The delegates roared.

There was also the old truism of what constitutes news, but with a twist: When a man bites a hot dog, it's not news, but when a hot dog bites a man, that's news. I also advised them on catchy headlines. When Secretary-General Ban Ki-moon complained there were over 1.3 billion people, mostly in the developing world, who live in virtual darkness because they have no access to electricity, our headline read: "Let there be light", says UN chief, "and there was darkness."

But Can You Type?
When the UN was long dominated by men, holding some of the highest positions in the staff hierarchy during most of its 75-

year existence, the overwhelming majority of women staffers were secretaries pounding on their typewriters seated outside their bosses' offices sheltered in cubicles. A story circulating at the UN for ages—perhaps going back to the proverbial Middle Ages – recounts a woman candidate being interviewed for a job. She had superlative credentials, including work experience as a political analyst and armed with a post-graduate degree from a prestigious Ivy League university in the US.

The male UN staffer from human resources, who interviewed her, had one jarring question: "But can you type?" Mercifully, that was in a bygone era. But since then, the UN has made significant progress trying to conform to an age-old General Assembly resolution calling for gender parity system wide.

The Two Bushes
When George W. Bush, the Governor of Texas and later US President, was unable to name the leaders of India, Pakistan and Chechnya in a newspaper interview, he was roasted by the news media for his ignorance on foreign policy issues. Bush, the son of former US President George Bush, also came under attack for mistakenly referring to Greeks as Grecians, East Timorese as East Timorians and for failing to distinguish between Slovakia and Slovenia. A cartoon in the New York Times showed the junior Bush, addressing the nation from a future White House, announcing plans to continue bombing Iraq while threatening Iraqi President Saddam Hussein.

"My fellow Americans," says Bush, unable to remember

either the country he is bombing or the leader under attack," "The bombing of the L-shaped country will continue, until its leader, what's-his-face with the mustache, agrees to something..."

In the background are two White House aides, one of whom whispers to the other: "He's misplaced his foreign policy index cards." But not all US politicians and presidents get their knowledge of foreign affairs from index cards handed over to them by their aides.

The senior George Bush, who was also head of Central Intelligence Agency (CIA), US Ambassador to the UN and the American envoy to China, had a prodigious knowledge of foreign affairs – in marked contrast to his son who, incidentally, held a bachelor's degree from Yale University and a master's from Harvard Business School. Still, as US President, he has ranked far ahead of Donald Trump and was never ridiculed as a moron or a pathological liar.

SRI LANKAN PERSPECTIVES

THE GOOD, THE BAD
&
THE NOT-SO-UGLY

CHAPTER 19

Left: Nandasiri Jasentuliyana, Chief of the Office of Outer Space Affairs at discussions on International Cooperation in Peaceful Uses of Outer Space.
Credit: United Nations

Rising from the Ocean Depths to Outer Space

When future historians take stock of Sri Lanka's enduring contributions at the United Nations, they may realize that our political legacy spanned both the upper and lower limits of the universe: the sky above and the oceans below. Shirley Amerasinghe was not only elected President of the General Assembly in September 1976 but also chaired the historic Law of the Sea (LOS) Conference which produced the ultimate treaty governing the ocean seabed and the high seas.

And both in 1982 and 1999, Nandasiri Jasentuliyana, an international expert on space law, was named Executive Secretary of the second and third UN Conferences on the Exploration and Peaceful Uses of Outer Space (UNISPACE II & III) that laid down the laws governing the heavenly skies preventing a possible arms race and a futuristic "Star Wars", Hollywood-style.

Still, between the deep blue sea and the wide-open skies, there was plenty of room for Sri Lankan success stories in terra firma: Dr Gamani Corea's two-term (1974-84) appointment as Secretary-General of the Geneva-based UN Conference on Trade and Development (UNCTAD); Andrew Joseph's short stint before retirement, as Associate Administrator of the UN Development Programme (UNDP) in 1989; Christopher Weeramantry's election as judge of the International Court of Justice (ICJ) in the Hague in 1991; and Jayantha Dhanapala's appointment as Under-Secretary-General for Disarmament Affairs in 1998.

An equally creditable achievement was the appointment in early 2006 of Radhika Coomaraswamy as Under-Secretary-General (USG) for Children in Armed Conflict. She became the fourth Sri Lankan to hold the post of a USG – the third highest-ranking position in the UN totem pole.

She was also the first Sri Lankan woman to rise to the higher echelons of the male-dominated UN Secretariat. If one is to take account of the genetic factor, she is perhaps a product of designer genes: her father Raju Coomaraswamy retired as an

Assistant Secretary-General and head of UNDP's Asian Bureau in the 1980s.

Radhika Coomaraswamy
Credit: United Nations

Blacklisted by a paranoid US Governor, who barred her from visiting women's prisons in the State of Michigan in 1998, Radhika later took on the mullahs of the Taliban-run government in Afghanistan. The Sri Lankan human rights activist, who was the UN's Special Rapporteur on Violence Against Women, was denied permission to visit three Michigan prisons facing accusations of widespread sexual misconduct against its women prisoners. The edict against her visit came from Michigan Governor John Engler.

Although Afghanistan is not a country held out as a model for Western democratic values, its rigidly Islamic Taliban government agreed to a visit by Radhika who was mandated by the UN to probe human rights violations in the politically troubled South Asian nation. After a two-week tour of Afghanistan and some of the refugee camps in neighbouring Pakistan, she said the Taliban's 'Department for the Promotion of Virtue and Prevention of Vice' is "the most misogynist entity in the world." Harsh words, no doubt, but she was right – judging by the mountainous negative reports on Afghanistan piling up at the UN.

Armed with superlative academic credentials, Radhika was one of the few – or perhaps the only – Sri Lankan triple Ivy Leaguer. A graduate of the UN International School in New York City, she received her B.A. from Yale University, her J.D. from Columbia and an LLM from Harvard.

Meanwhile, when Sri Lanka (then Ceylon) gained admission to the United Nations back in December 1955, the first-ever mission to the U.N. was literally homeless. As the former Ambassador to the U.S. Neville Kanakaratne would recount, our application for membership was vetoed by the then Soviet Union on the ground that we still had a defence agreement with the United Kingdom (and that Trincomalee was a naval base under the control of the British, despite our independence in February 1948). The charge was that we were NOT a truly independent nation-state – but still a British colony.

Therefore, the Soviets argued, Sri Lanka did not warrant a seat in the world body. The truth of the matter, however, was that we were caught up in the politics of the Cold War and were victims of a Soviet ideological battle with the West. The Western powers, in turn, kept vetoing Soviet allies barring them from UN membership.

As part of a package deal, however, we gained admission in December 1995 in return for the US holding back its veto on Soviet allies such as Albania, Bulgaria, Hungary, and Romania, who eventually made it to the UN the same day as we did. Although we were knocking at the UN door since 1950, it took five long years to gain admission.

The swift admission in 1955, however, took the government by mild surprise, with no immediate office space to house the new Sri Lanka Mission to the UN. The Good Samaritan came in the guise of Lawrence Gunatilaka, a trail-blazing Sri Lankan who had arrived in the US in the early 1950s, and who offered his apartment in the service of his country. Gunatilaka's apartment in West 73rd street was the first home of the Sri Lankan Mission to the United Nations. The mailing address of the apartment even adorned the first set of letterheads printed by the Mission. Ambassador Kanakaratne said: "Lawrence's apartment was the headquarters for about two to three months until we found a brownstone in Sutton Place."

The first Permanent Representative to the U.N., Sir Senerat (RSS) Gunewardene, had to shuttle between New York and Washington DC because his assignment as ambassador to the U.S. took precedence over the United Nations. We were perpetually short of delegates during the annual General Assembly sessions. But by the late 1970s, we had a glut of delegates, with hordes of MPs and politicians arriving in New York, as part of a refresher course in international politics.

During a crucial voting, however, most of the MP-delegates were missing from their seats – and were later tracked down to a then-famous discount appliance stores in Canal Street in lower Manhattan, where they were on a shopping spree. Travel not only broadened their minds but also their suitcases.

Shirley Amerasinghe was the first Sri Lankan who made himself available for the post of UN Secretary-General back in

1971. "Strictly speaking", said Kumar Chitty, Special Assistant to the Special Representative at the Law of the Sea secretariat, Amerasinghe was "not against" (then Secretary-General) Kurt Waldheim, but he had informed Waldheim that he would make himself available "if needed." When he ran for a third term as Secretary-General, Waldheim was vetoed 16 times and was later succeeded by Javier Perez de Cuellar.

Chitty, later Assistant Secretary-General (ASG) and Registrar of the Law of the Sea Tribunal in Hamburg, said that Amerasinghe was the official candidate of Sri Lanka "to the extent that the Foreign Ministry delegation to the General Assembly sessions (at that time) did go around indicating he was available and had the support of the Government". There was no official announcement of candidature. And there wasn't the type of political lobbying that goes on nowadays, said Chitty.

But according to speculation, Amerasinghe was branded as "too pro-Palestinian" and therefore unable to win the support of the US and other Western powers. When the Al Aqsa Mosque in Jerusalem was burnt triggering protests Israel, he was one of the keynote speakers during the Middle East debate in the Security Council. He later became the first chairman of the three-member Israeli Practices Committee (which documented Israeli human rights violations in occupied territories).

That perhaps was one of the final blows that gutted his chances in the run-up to the election for a new Secretary-General in a country where the Israeli lobby reigns supreme.

He got pretty close to Waldheim's total in the first count but was blocked by a veto – possibly cast by the Americans, according to Nandasiri (Nandi) Jasentuliyana, then a staff member of the UN secretariat and later Deputy Director-General, UN Office in Vienna and Director of the UN Office for Outer Space Affairs.

Nandi said that most notable in that period was the influence of Sri Lanka's Permanent Representatives, including Sir Senarat (who held the post twice in 1958 and 1963) and later Sir Claude Corea and Shirley Amerasinghe, who had unfettered access to the upper echelons of the UN Secretariat.

When the second UN Secretary-General Dag Hammarskjold of Sweden died in a mysterious plane crash in the Congo in 1961, Ambassador Kanakaratne was a Legal Adviser in the Secretariat. Hammarskjold's trouble-shooting UN team to Congo was to have included a Legal Adviser.

At the eleventh hour, Kanakaratne decided to back out of the trip because he thought his knowledge of French was relatively poor compared to that of Vladmir Fabri, another UN Legal Adviser. Fabri took Kanakaratne's place on that fateful plane that crashed in the Congo, killing the entire delegation.

As Kanakaratne told me, the 'Ceylon Observer' ran a lead story with the headline: "Was Our Man on the Death Plane." "Somebody had taken the newspaper to my mother – and she almost collapsed," Kanakaratne recalled. Within 24 hours, the record was set straight by our Permanent Representative at that time, Ambassador Gunapala Malalasekera (1961-1963).

Speaking of newspaper headlines, the first reporter to cover the UN back in 1956 was Ernest Corea, onetime editor of both the Daily News and the Observer, and later Sri Lanka's Ambassador to the US. Ed Kerner, a former Sri Lankan Director of Tourism in New York, covered the UN in the early 1970s for a short-lived Hongkong-based newspaper called the "Asian" edited by the legendary Tarzie Vittachi, a longtime editor of the Observer.

Tarzie once offered me a piece of advice: "Don't ever join the UN," he warned, "They will take a journalist and make a bureaucrat out of you." Still, he himself fought against that very bureaucracy and was one of the few – or perhaps the only high-ranking UN official – who continued his journalistic career, as a columnist for Newsweek magazine, even when he was Deputy Executive Director of the UN children's agency UNICEF holding the rank of a UN assistant secretary-general.

Review and Extension Conference of the Treaty on Non-Proliferation of Nuclear Weapons Opens at UN HQ. Seated on the podium from left to right are: Secretary-General Boutros Boutros-Ghali; Ambassador Jayantha Dhanapala (Sri Lanka), President of the Conference; Prvoslav Davinic, Secretary-General of the Conference. Credit: United Nations

As a strong advocate of development journalism and supportive of a Third World news agency, Tarzie backed IPS news agency to the hilt and provided a strong partnership with the UN Population Fund (UNFPA) when he was Director of Communications there. After his retirement, he was a frequent visitor to our office. During one of his visits, he was very critical of the Sri Lanka government at that time and lashed out at some of our leaders. As he was leaving our office, he turned back, looked at me seated at my desktop, and said: "When you are writing my obituary, make sure you mention that". And I did.

Meanwhile, Jayantha Dhanapala, a former U.N. under-secretary-general for disarmament affairs (1998-2003) and a relentless advocate for a world free of nuclear weapons, was the recipient of the 2014 International Achievement Award for Nuclear Disarmament sponsored by Inter Press Service (IPS) news agency.

"Short of actually dismantling nuclear devices himself," said Dr. Randy Rydell, former senior political affairs officer at the U.N. Office for Disarmament Affairs (UNODA), "he has contributed enormously to constructing a solid foundation upon which the world community will one day fulfill this great ambition."

A one-time President of the Nobel Prize-winning Pugwash Conferences on Science and World Affairs (since 2007) and a former Sri Lankan ambassador to the United States, Jayantha played a crucial role in the 1995 Conference of States Parties to the Treaty on the Non-Proliferation of Nuclear Weapons (NPT).

The award – which was co-sponsored by the Tokyo-based Soka Gakkai International (SGI), a 12-million-strong, lay Buddhist non-governmental organization (NGO) which has been leading a global campaign for the abolition of nuclear weapons – was presented at an official ceremony at the United Nations Nov. 17, 2014.

Douglas Roche, a former senator, an ex-Canadian ambassador for disarmament, and visiting professor at the University of Alberta, told IPS, "When the Non-Proliferation Treaty was indefinitely extended in 1995, the person most responsible for making nuclear disarmament a permanent legal obligation was Ambassador Jayantha Dhanapala."

He said Jayantha's "masterful diplomacy" – threading a course between the powerful nuclear weapons states and the non-nuclear world – was responsible for delineating three specific promises. First, the systematic and progressive efforts towards the elimination of nuclear weapons; second, a Comprehensive Nuclear Test Ban Treaty by 1996; third, an early conclusion of negotiations for a fissile material ban.

CHAPTER 20

Prime Minister SWRD Bandaranaike during his visit to the UN to address the General Assembly in 1956. Credit: UN photo

When Little Lanka Roared in Defence of the UN

When Sri Lanka (then Ceylon) was a fledgeling member of the United Nations back in the late 1950s, the expatriate community in New York was so minuscule that the Sri Lanka Association could have held its annual general meeting in a street-corner phone booth.

Our first attempt at seeking membership was in May 1948 – three months after independence. The application was signed by D.S. Senanayake, the country's first Prime Minister, who also held the portfolio of Minister for External Affairs.

But unfortunately, we got embroiled in big power politics,

not of our choosing. The application was rejected by the Security Council where the USSR used its veto against us. The Council resolution said it "resolves to postpone" the decision of our admission until there was "sufficient proof that Ceylon is a sovereign and independent state."

Sensing the deadlock, Prime Minister Sir John Kotelawela handpicked Esmond Wickremesinghe, a media mogul, and a consummate political power broker, anointing him as a Special Envoy, with a single-minded mandate: to lobby US and Soviet diplomats for a politically smooth passage for admission to the world body.

Esmond, father of former Prime Minister Ranil Wickremesinghe, was not only a highly influential press magnate of outstanding stature, but also a political kingmaker and a skilled behind-the-scenes negotiator. With strong support from R.S.S. Gunewardene, (who later became our first Permanent Representative to the UN), Esmond played a key role in successfully negotiating a "package deal".

Ernest Corea, a former editor of the Ceylon Daily News and the Observer, and who worked closely under Esmond at Lake House, said Sir John rewarded Esmond with an offer of a knighthood: a deserving title of Sir Esmond Wickremesinghe. But Esmond apparently turned it down – and the knighthood went to R.S.S. Gunewardene, later Sir Senerath Gunewardene.

Even as Managing Director of the Associated Newspapers Ceylon Ltd, Esmond always kept out of the limelight – even instructing all his editors never to publish his photo or feature him in any of the Lake House newspapers.

Our admission to the UN only proved his skills as a successful negotiator – away from the public eye. Sir John, unfortunately, did not get to make the planned "grand entry" at the UN because the UNP was swept aside by a political landslide in 1956 and S.W.R.D. Bandaranaike, the new SLFP prime minister, headed the country's delegation to the 1956/57 sessions of the General Assembly. And according to Ernest, Bandaranaike made his first and last appearance at the UN where he had the distinction of speaking extempore before an Assembly where most leaders read out a prepared text or more recently employed a teleprompter.

Ernest, later a Sri Lankan Ambassador to the US, covered the first General Assembly sessions for the Lake House group of newspapers in late 1956. He recalled the inspiring, off-the-cuff speech made by Prime Minister S.W.R.D. Bandaranaike when he led the first Sri Lankan delegation to the UN in November 1956.

He said that many delegates were astonished by the Prime Minister's eloquence. "Then, as now, most UN speeches were bureaucratic, drafted by functionaries and read out by those who cannot function adequately at a podium. SWRD broke that mold. He was an orator rather than a "speaker" or reader. He represented an authentic Asian viewpoint with clarity, sharpness, and wit."

As it is today, the Middle East was an international hotspot at that time following Egyptian President Gamal Abdel Nasser's decision to nationalize the Suez Canal Company after the US and Britain had humiliated him by blocking a World Bank loan for the construction of the Aswan High Dam.

Nasser's decision eventually provoked a strong military reaction from Britain and France, which jointly administered the Suez Canal, forcing UN intervention. And around the same time, the then Soviet Union invaded Hungary provoking an equally strong reaction in the corridors of power at the UN.

The role of the UN came under harsh scrutiny at that time, as it was later in Iraq and Afghanistan. Is the UN a helpless giant or a toothless tiger? UN Secretary-General Kofi Annan's defence of the UN in 2003 may well have come off the pages of Bandaranaike's five-page speech to the General Assembly in 1956.

The events in Egypt and Hungary, Bandaranaike told delegates, had provided a crucial test and an opportunity to the UN. "I should like to say that it is my opinion that the United Nations has emerged out of these crises with its reputation and prestige enhanced. I have heard, no doubt, many people here criticize the United Nations on the grounds that it is slow to act, that when it does act, it cannot act effectively, that it sometimes tends to lose itself in diffused thinking-and still more diffused decisions."

Bandaranaike also said something that Annan kept repeating in later years: that the UN has limited power and authority, particularly in the face of unilateral action by Western nations.

As Bandaranaike put it: "The United Nations is not a superstate possessed of armed forces capable of asserting its authority even over powerful members or non-members who may act contrary to the purposes of the United Nations. It can and does bring to bear a certain collective moral force of the world which, although it may not be expeditiously effective in all cases, commands in certain cases, as it has done in the past, success and in certain others at least a very salutary restraining influence."

In his address to the Assembly, he also had the courage of his conviction to defend Nasser's decision to take over the Suez Canal, which rightfully belonged to Egypt. "The President of Egypt nationalized the Suez Canal Company. I do not find in any quarter a disposition seriously to question his right to do so. Although the manner in which it was done, the time in which it was done, may be considered expedient by some and incorrect by others, the basic fact of his right to do so has not been questioned," Bandaranaike said.

If that is correct, he said, "I consider that it follows as a corollary to the nationalization of the Suez Canal Company that the power of operation of the canal should also be vested in Egypt."

In an Assembly where you rarely hear religious injunctions, Bandaranaike harked back to Buddhist scriptures to fault delegates for launching attacks at each other. "We gain nothing," he said, "by undue mutual recriminations and reviling. As a Buddhist, I remember the story of Buddha and the answer he gave to an opponent who came before him and abused him for hours."

The Buddha listened to him patiently and said: "My dear friend, if you invite guests to a banquet and the guests do not come, what do you do with the food that is prepared?" 'Oh, my family and I will consume the food," the man responded. So, the Buddha said to the man who had abused him: "You have offered me your abuse. I am not accepting it. You can take it yourself."

CHAPTER 21

Credit: United Nations

How an Intruder in the General Assembly was Upstaged by a Foreign Minister

Sri Lanka had its fair share of Foreign Ministers who made their annual visits to the UN during the General Assembly sessions in September when the world body traditionally hosted over 150 world leaders, including heads of state and heads of government.

Sri Lanka's Foreign Minister ACS Hameed had one of his memorable moments when an Eelam activist and lawyer from London, Krishna Vaikunthavasan, surreptitiously gate-crashed into the UN and tried to upstage Hameed by walking onto the podium of the General Assembly hall and momentarily took the speaker's slot.

The incident, perhaps a rarity in the history of the UN, saw the intruder unleashing a diatribe against a member state accusing it of genocide and lambasting the government for committing war crimes against the Tamils fighting for a separate state in northern Sri Lanka.

When the president of the Assembly realized he had an interloper on his hands, he cut off the mike and summoned security guards who bodily ejected him from the hall and banned him from the UN premises. And as Hameed walked up to the podium, there was pin-drop silence in the Assembly Hall.

As a member of the Sri Lanka delegation at that time, I was seated behind Hameed. But the unflappable Hameed, unprompted by any of his delegates, produced a riveting punchline: "Mr. President", he said "I want to thank the previous speaker for keeping his speech short," he said, as the Assembly, known to suffer longwinded speeches, broke into peals of laughter. The intruder was in effect upstaged by the Foreign Minister.

Hameed's canny sense of humor also went far beyond the confines of the UN. When he came under attack for staying in five-star luxury hotels during the UN General Assembly sessions in New York, he fired back at the Opposition MP in Parliament with a rejoinder dripping with sarcasm: "Where do you want me to stay when I travel overseas as the Foreign

Minister?", he asked. "in thosai boutiques?"

To put it in perspective, that would be like rooming at the Ambal Café in Hulftsdorf or Saraswathy Lodge in Bambalapitya. Or perhaps Saravana Bhavan in New York's Lexington Avenue.

Hameed routinely pitched his tent either at New York's Hyatt Regency, the Intercontinental Barclay, the Waldorf Astoria or the Palace Hotel—and he did it in style, like scores of other high-flying Foreign Ministers arriving for the UN sessions. A globe-trotter of near-biblical proportions, he was probably in Colombo only on transit, in between catching overseas flights.

Hameed was an unforgettable character in his heyday—enjoying every single moment of his tenure as Foreign Minister beginning 1977. And more so, because President JR Jayewardene (JRJ) never addressed the UN nor stepped into the UN premises (even while he stayed at the Waldorf Astoria in New York during his state visit to Washington DC in April 1983.) The reasons for shunning the UN remains a mystery.

With Sri Lanka holding the chairmanship of the Non-Aligned Movement (NAM) during 1976-1979, Hameed was constantly called upon to preside over some of the thorniest international issues of the mid-1970s: which of the two Cambodian factions had the rightful claim to the seat at the UN (the General Assembly session that day was held up for over four hours as he negotiated behind closed doors to help resolve the dispute, with backing from the UN's Legal Adviser)? Was it Kampuchea under the Khmer Rouge regime (1975-1979)?

And, in another dispute, should Egypt, which had signed

the Camp David peace agreement with Israel in 1978, be driven out of NAM? There were also sharp divisions in NAM over the disputed territory of Western Sahara in the Maghreb region of North Africa and the split over the Soviet invasion of Afghanistan (1979-1989).

As he sat in judgement, Hameed's closest advisers during the General Assembly sessions included two outstanding career diplomats, Jayantha Dhanapala and Nihal Rodrigo, along with Ernest Corea, Sri Lanka's High Commissioner to Canada and later Ambassador to the United States.

Ernest was one of Hameed's longstanding friends, having known him long before he became Foreign Minister, and was the only Sri Lankan Ambassador who addressed him by his first name: Shahul, throwing protocol to the winds.

As Ernest once told me: "Shahul faced many challenges in his life – one of them was a lack of physical height – but his biggest challenge was managing the Foreign Affairs portfolio for the Sri Lanka government. To the best of my recollection, he was the first Foreign Minister to hold that portfolio without the direct involvement of the Prime Minister's/President's office". Previously, Defence and External Affairs were integrated into a single portfolio.

When President Jayewardene unhitched them, there was a widespread perception, particularly in Colombo's foreign policy establishment, that the whole business of foreign affairs was being downgraded. "Shahul proved them wrong", said Ernest.

As part of the landscape in the UN Delegate's Lounge, Hameed was seen holding court, even as he kept chomping at his cigar, probably the best from Cuba, which he picked up in Havana during his frequent trips to the Cuban capital, before Sri Lanka handed over the NAM chairmanship to Fidel Castro in 1979.

At home, Hameed had a tough task steering the NAM ship among sceptics like Gamini Dissanayake and Lalith Athulathmudali, and of course, JRJ himself. Still, Hameed showed remarkable patience and persistence.

Perhaps his most joyous moment as Foreign Minister was when JRJ told Fidel Castro at the Havana summit that it was Hameed who enabled Sri Lanka to hand over NAM's leadership to Cuba "untarnished and unaltered."

This put to rest the speculation even within his own party that his days as Foreign Minister would be short. "The fact is that JRJ realized as few others did that Shahul had an intuitive feel for international relations. Those who had the privilege of working with him understood this. He had his faults. Who doesn't?" asked Ernest.

"I am not going to be counted among his critics who might want to let fly at him now that he is no longer with us. Rather, I would like to remind those of us who worked with him and others who observed him at work that he was outstanding in several areas".

First, he was tri-lingual: in English, Sinhala, and Tamil. This gave him a remarkable reputation among his peers. Second, he had a phenomenal memory and could at precisely the correct moment during a drafting session pull out from the recesses of his mind a word, a phrase or other salient reference that added substance and depth to a public policy statement. He was also insistent, as some of his colleagues were not, that a solid Sri Lanka/India relationship was an essential component of foreign policy, said Ernest.

"One more point needs to be stressed, and this is very personal. He was an excellent extempore speaker. He could intervene in a debate to deal with a complex issue for which most of us were unprepared as if he was saying to himself: "Here's that loose ball I was waiting for," declared Ernest.

Armed with self-deprecating humour, Hameed funded the publication of a collection of cartoons that lampooned him. He particularly relished a cartoon which showed him sitting before a huge globe with the caption: "Let me see – what are the countries I have still not visited." His initials ACS were spelled out as "All Countries Seen."

An equally lovable cartoon in November 1978 showed a world-weary Hameed arriving at the Katunayake airport and innocently asking a passer-by: "My dear man, could you show me the way to Harispattuwa?," his electorate in his hometown of Akurana, a majority Sinhala Buddhist electorate. And to have been elected over a very long period was a tribute to Hameed's political relationship among his voters.

The cartoons were sketches from some of Sri Lanka's celebrated artists of the 1970s, including W.R.Wijesoma,

Jiffrey Yoonoos, Mark Gerreyn and Amita Abayesekera."One of the greatest gifts is the ability to laugh at oneself," said Wijesoma in an introduction to the book titled "Mr Foreign Minister", " Mr Hameed is doing just that, and I believe he is having the last laugh." Oscar Wilde once made the distinction between two forms of torture: the rack and the Press. Ask any politician, said Hameed, and he would opt for the grisly torture chamber over the editorial offices and the news desks in Colombo.

CHAPTER 22

Sri Lankan Envoys in US Walking on Tight Ropes

When a senior career diplomat was offered a new posting as Ambassador to the United States back in 2009, he gracefully declined the offer. In a private conversation, "strictly off-the-record and not-for-attribution", he told me: "Being a Sri Lankan ambassador in Washington DC is like walking on a tight rope with the bucket of s –-t on your head."

Perhaps he was notoriously right because the government at that time was virtually "blacklisted" by the US and battling charges of human rights violations, civilian killings, and war crimes in northern Sri Lanka. The task ahead for any envoy was not only to deny these killings but also to justify atrocities if any.

Over the years, governments of all political hues sustained a longstanding tradition of appointing retired and aging former military chiefs* – including Generals, Air Marshals and

Brigadiers – as ambassadors and high commissioners overseas. A senior career diplomat, with an offbeat sense of humor, posed what seemed like a logical question: "if former army chiefs can be appointed as ambassadors, why shouldn't former ambassadors be appointed as army chiefs."

At a farewell dinner for Major General Shavendra Silva, Deputy Permanent Representative to the UN with Ambassadorial rank (2010-2015), later promoted to General and Commander of the Armed Forces, I predicted that Shavendra will be the first Sri Lankan ambassador in history who will be appointed Army Chief. And I was right, proving the argument why former diplomats shouldn't be appointed army chiefs.

Like most foreign services worldwide, Sri Lanka has two categories of diplomats: career diplomats and political appointees. When career diplomats reach the retiring age of 55-60, they are forced into retirement. But are no such age limits on political appointees, mostly in their late 60s, 70s or even 80s. Perhaps by accident or by design, some of our aging political envoys accredited to Egypt died in office –- prompting an Egyptian Foreign Ministry official to tell a visiting Sri Lankan official: "The only thing older than your ambassadors are our pyramids". Forget pre-historic mummies.

Which reminds me: When Mrs. Sirimavo Bandaranaike, the world's first woman Prime Minister (who served three terms: 1960 –1965, 1970 –1977 and 1994 –2000), addressed a summit meeting of the Non-Aligned Movement (NAM) in Belgrade in

1961, she reportedly made a newsworthy speech with a riveting opening para: "As a mother and a Prime Minister." And years later she was due to address another NAM meeting, this time in the Egyptian capital of Cairo in 1964.

As the delegates holed up in a hotel, overlooking the pyramids, were racking their brains for another catchy opening line, Felix Dias Bandaranaike, then a cabinet minister and a member of the Sri Lanka delegation, jokingly suggested the lead para for the speech: "As a mummy and as a Prime Minister". Mrs. Bandaranaike apparently wasn't amused – and what saved Felix from losing his Cabinet portfolio was he was a close relative.

Incidentally, a visiting emissary, a Foreign Minister from an Asian country, was in Sri Lanka to personally invite our Prime Minister for an upcoming Non-Aligned summit meeting scheduled to take place in an Asian capital. As he listed the names of some of the world's leaders who were scheduled to address the meeting, our Prime Minister, who was obviously ignorant of the basics of the Non-Aligned Movement, asked the visiting minister: "So, who is coming from America?" much to the embarrassment of the Foreign Minister. A US President at a NAM summit?

Ambassador Nihal Rodrigo, a diplomat with an offbeat sense of humor going back to his undergraduate days at Peradeniya where we had adjacent rooms at Marrs Hall, was one of the earliest proponents of the Non-Aligned Movement (NAM). Perhaps he was more than a foot soldier pounding the corridors and committee rooms at the UN keeping track of the inner workings of the Coordinating Bureau of NAM based at the UN. At the Foreign Ministry, as one career diplomat told me, nothing on NAM would get traction unless and until approved by Nihal.

When he collapsed, totally exhausted, after a 24-hour stint at the BIMCH, just ahead of a NAM summit meeting, he apparently told his first responders: "Never mind me. Save the Movement," as he was carried out on a stretcher, according to widespread unconfirmed rumors at that time.

And so, it was appropriate that India's Permanent Representative to the UN Brajesh Mishra (1979-81), once paid him a supreme backhanded compliment when he called Nihal "the running dog of Non-Alignment." It certainly beat the North Koreans lambasting Western leaders as "running dogs of Imperialism".

Meanwhile, some of the political appointees were also not very savvy – either politically or diplomatically. A Sri Lankan UNICEF official based in the Bangladeshi capital of Dhaka recounted a story about a visiting Sri Lankan official from the Food and Agriculture Organization (FAO) in Rome. As the usual gesture among Sri Lankans posted overseas, the UNICEF official arranged for a meeting between the Sri Lankan Ambassador, a political appointee, and the visiting FAO official.

At the meeting in the envoy's office, the UNICEF official discovered the ambassador had obviously not done his homework: he was not only ignorant of what the FAO was all about but, worst of all, he did not even know what the acronym FAO stood for. During the course of the conversation, the envoy asked the FAO official what his area of specialization was. Told he was in charge of a division overseeing fisheries, the envoy's eyes lit up, this time with a personal request: "I say, can you get me some Maldive fish." Perhaps transmitted via the UN diplomatic pouch from FAO to Dhaka...

In the Sri Lankan diplomatic service there is never a dull moment. Or so it seems. There was the hilarious story of a newly appointed Ambassador, accredited to an Asian country, who downgraded his brother-in-law to the rank of a cook (mercifully not a crook) just to include him as a member of his staff so that the Foreign Ministry can pick up the tab for his travel and his upkeep.

And then there was a Foreign Minister whose sister-in-law, brother-in-law and intended daughter-in-law were all assigned diplomatic appointments in different world capitals. The joke in ministry circles was that when he ran out of "in-laws" he was looking for "out-laws" in his family circle.

Meanwhile, at least one school in Colombo had the rare distinction of producing two UN Permanent Representatives (PRUNs) from two different countries. Ambassador Ahmed Zaki (1979-83) of the Maldives and Ambassador Ben Fonseka of Sri Lanka (1980-84) who were contemporaries at the UN in the 1980s. And they were products of what Americans call a high school: St Peter's College, Wellawatte.

Footnote

Over the years, the military chiefs who were appointed Ambassadors and High Commissioners included the following:

- General (Rtrd) Rohan Daluwatte, RWP, RSP, VSV, USP - Ambassador to Brazil
- General (Rtrd) Deshamanya D. S. Attygalle, MVO - High Commissioner to United Kingdom
- General (Rtrd) G. H. De Silva, RWP, RSP, VSV, USP - High Commissioner to Pakistan
- General (Rtrd) Deshamanya Denis Perera, VSV - High Commissioner to Australia
- General (Rtrd) Shantha Kottegoda, WWV, RWP, RSP, VSV, USP - Ambassador to Brazil and Thailand
- Major General (Rtrd) Nanda Mallawaarachchi, RWP, VSV, USP - Ambassador to Indonesia
- Major General (Rtrd) Anton Muttukumaru, OBE, ED, ADC - High Commissioner to Australia, New Zealand, Pakistan, and Ambassador to Egypt
- Major General (Rtrd) Janaka Perera, RWP, RSP, VSV, USP - High Commissioner to Australia & Ambassador to Indonesia
- General (Rtrd) Cyril Ranatunga, VSV - High Commissioner to Australia and United Kingdom
- Major General (Rtrd) Richard Udugama, MBE - Ambassador to Iraq
- General (Rtrd) Cecil Waidyaratne, VSV, USP, SLAC - Ambassador to Thailand

- General (Rtrd) C. S. Weerasooriya, RWP, RSP, VSV, USP - High Commissioner to Pakistan
- General (Rtrd) T. I. Weerathunga, VSV - High Commissioner to Canada
- General (Rtrd) Jagath Jayasuriya, RWP, VSV, USP - Ambassador to Brazil

Source: Wikipedia

CHAPTER 23

Sri Lankan journalists covering JRJ's visit to the US in June 1984

Advice to Besieged Delegates:
Get the Hell Out of the UN

Come September, every Sri Lankan President and Prime Minister routinely visited New York to address the annual sessions of the UN General Assembly. In the case of the Bandaranaike's, three generations addressed the UN, including Prime Ministers SWRD Bandaranaike (1956-59), his wife Sirimavo Bandaranaike and their daughter President Chandrika Bandaranaike Kumaratunga (CBK). But they were not the first "first family" to achieve that distinction because India joined the privileged ranks with the Nehru family, first Prime Minister

Pandit Jawaharlal Nehru (1947-64), then daughter Indira Gandhi followed by son Rajiv Gandhi.

Among Sri Lankan leaders, President JR Jayewardene (Junius Richard Jayewardene, affectionately called "Dicky" by his family) was a rare exception because, for some unaccountable reason, he never addressed the UN, nor did he step into the Secretariat building although he broke journey in New York, staying at the Waldorf Astoria, following his state visit to the White House in June 1984. Did he think the UN was a colossal failure? Or was the UN an exercise in political futility? No one had an answer.

During President JRJ's visit to the US in 1984, most TV newscasters got their pronunciations wrong—Jayewar-deen instead of Jaye- wardene'. So, when my American friends and colleagues asked me whether I was related to the visiting president, I told them with a straight face: "Yes. Our President is Jayewar-deen, and I am Thalif Deen—and he is my uncle." As the comedian Woody Allen would say: "They bought it". I told this to JRJ when I interviewed him at the Waldorf Astoria. And he laughed.

The scene shifts to Geneva where a Sri Lankan delegation, led by JRJ's brother HW Jayewardene (HWJ), an eminent lawyer, was discussing a strategy to beat a proposed Western-inspired resolution aimed at condemning Sri Lanka for human rights violations during its battle against the Tamil separatist movement in the north. The resolution was expected to come up before the Geneva-based Human Rights Council – even as our delegates were holed up in a hotel room late into the night trying to figure out how best to upstage the sponsors.

During the middle of the discussion close to midnight (Geneva time), HWJ called his brother Dicky in Colombo for advice as to how best to beat the move by Western powers. The tail-end of the conversation, as reported by delegates who were privy to the phone call, went as follows: "Yes Dicky, Yes Dicky, No Dicky, you can't do that, Dicky." After hanging up the phone, HWJ turned to the delegates and said: "He wants us to get out of the UN".

Meanwhile, every Sri Lankan delegation included the country's Foreign Minister, some impressive and knowledgeable and others not-so-impressive and ignorant of international affairs. At least one Foreign Minister was caught fast asleep on his wife's shoulder as he occupied the Sri Lankan seat in one of the front rows on the General Assembly hall—an act considered a diplomatic insult, and more so because the speaker at the podium was the Foreign Minister of India. Luckily, he did not snore because he may have woken up some of his delegates seated behind him.

But what our Foreign Minister did not realize was that several news photographers, located high up in the Assembly Hall, were taking shots with telephoto lenses. When a Japanese newspaper ran the photograph, all hell broke loose at the Foreign Ministry (or as the Americans say: the s—t hit the fan). And the then Director of Public Relations, Kshenuka Senewiratne, was assigned the unenviable task of appealing to newspaper editors in Colombo to kill both the story and the photo. She did an admirable job because only one newspaper ran the photo, but it was buried in one of the inside pages.

And then there was a story of a Foreign Minister summoning an urgent meeting of his senior staff to cope with a hostage crisis, of all places in Siberia, where our workers were being held for ransom or in danger of being killed. But the puzzled officials looked at each other. Siberia? Sri Lankan hostages? It apparently didn't make any sense until one of the officials who had read about a hostage crisis in Africa asked the Minister: "Sir, are your sure it was Siberia and not Liberia". "I say, Siberia? Liberia? What's the difference? They are all the same," he retorted. Perhaps he should have received a crash course in geography when he visited the UN for the next General Assembly sessions.

Meanwhile a visiting Foreign Minister was in New York at a time when there were reports of a possible reconciliation between the government and the Liberation Tigers of Tamil Eelam (LTTE). And equally significant was the rumor that if the peace negotiations succeeded, the LTTE fighters were expected to be absorbed into the Sri Lankan armed forces.

Asked to confirm, he said, "Yes", and jokingly added, "if that happens, we can some send some of our suicide bombers on UN peacekeeping missions." And then added: "But don't quote me on that" And this was a time when Sri Lanka was dispatching hundreds of our troops on UN peacekeeping missions to Africa and central America.

Meanwhile, when the General Assembly ousted Taiwan from the UN and admitted mainland China into the world body back in September 1971, a cartoonist for a London daily flipped the old cliché "a bull in a china shop" into "china in a bull shop."

The late Mervyn de Silva, known for his prodigious knowledge of foreign affairs, rightly realized China's potential as a major political, economic and military power. Sharp-witted and cynical, he always remained amused by the red baiting that went on in the US during the height of the Cold War in the 1950s when the virulently anti-Communist Senator Joseph R. McCarthy was "looking for reds under every bed."

When he was editor of the Daily News in the late 1960s, Mervyn discovered that the mostly American and British wire service stories reproduced in his own newspaper kept referring to China as "Red China." In the American political lexicon, "red" denoted radicalism, anarchy and Communism – at times, all three rolled into one.

Reprimanding his copy editors, Mervyn sent a note to the foreign desk of the Daily News advising his staff that there was only one China. – and that "Red China" was a figment in the minds of Western journalists. "China is China," he said, "And I don't want 850 million people (currently 1.3 billion) reduced to a piece of crimson coloured crockery."

Shirley Temple Black, one of Hollywood's iconic movie stars, later US ambassador to Ghana and Czechoslovakia, and who represented the US at the UN General Assembly sessions in 1969, was once asked what she thought of "Red China". In a response, dripping with sarcasm, she told reporters: "I think it will look good on a yellow tablecloth."

CHAPTER 24

An Envoy's Offer of a "Confidential" File Came With a Catch

As one of Sri Lanka's hot-shot criminal lawyers, Daya Perera was not only gifted with oratorical skills but also a devastating sense of humour. At the United Nations, where he had a post-legal career as Sri Lanka's Permanent Representative (1988-1991), he had a field day unleashing both his skills with the force of a double-barreled shotgun.

By sheer accident, the very first day Daya walked into the UN, he was pressed into service on an unexpected assignment as acting President of the General Assembly since Sri Lanka was one of the vice presidents at that time. Chairing the UN's highest policy-making body on his maiden visit to the UN, Daya emerged unscathed after his baptism of diplomatic fire.

As he climbed down the podium at the conclusion of the afternoon's session, the irrepressible Daya turned to one of his deputies and said: "This is the first time I spoke without charging a fee." At home, he was known not only for his outstanding successes in criminal court but also for his premium legal fees. The only clients who could afford him were apparently the super-rich – and denizens of the criminal underworld.

The United Nations was perhaps the only institution where, for the first time in his professional career, he grudgingly practiced the art of "free" speech — literally and metaphorically. At his farewell dinner at a five-star hotel in New York, one of the speakers jokingly said that Daya's annual income was far higher than the entire gross domestic product (GDP) of the Maldives – -even as the Maldivian ambassador present at the dinner nodded his head in mock agreement.

At one of the first diplomatic receptions he attended, he met the Ambassador from the Caribbean island of Belize. The envoy had also just arrived for his assignment at the United Nations. Asked for his profession, the ambassador told Daya he was a dentist. And when he asked Daya for his profession, he couldn't resist the temptation of telling the Belizean with good-humored grace: "Ambassador, you make money out of other people's mouths, I make money out of my own mouth."

Since journalists and diplomats are perpetually looking for inside stories, political gossip, and breaking news, I built a strong working relationship with Daya during his tenure as Ambassador. When I was in his office one day, he dropped a file marked "Confidential" before me.

To me, it looked like a journalist's dream because the file was expected to contain, not only Sri Lanka's official stance on some of the politically sensitive issues, but also letters detailing the running battle he had with the Foreign Secretary in Colombo, who was one of Daya's bosses.

Just when I thought I may have a series of journalistic scoops, he remarked in characteristic Sri Lankan idiom: "You bugger, you can read, but you cannot write". I told him: "Daya, you are treating me like a eunuch in a Middle Eastern harem. I can see all what's going on, but I cannot do anything myself." He appreciated that wisecrack. In tempting me with the "Confidential" file, he was not only making a gesture symbolizing our friendship but also refusing to betray the trust his government had placed on him as a senior high-ranking diplomat at the UN.

During voting time at the UN, ambassadors routinely stick to the advice or instructions from the Foreign Ministry in Colombo. But when the voting is by secret ballot, it is difficult to enforce this rule. When Daya's relationship with the Foreign Ministry soured, he told me: "My government can give be instructions on how to vote. But my vote will depend on the relationships I build with other ambassadors here."

As Sri Lanka's Permanent Representative, Daya chaired the Ad Hoc Committee on the Indian Ocean (while being conscious of an Indian ambassador's statement that many Americans erroneously think the Indian Ocean belongs to India) and also headed the U.N. Committee on Israeli Practices (also referred to as Israeli Malpractices Committee) dealing with human rights violations in the Occupied Territories.

As chairman of that Committee, he held court at least twice a year, in Amman, Damascus and Cairo, where Palestinians lamented the sufferings they underwent in Israeli occupied territories in Gaza and the West Bank. A strong supporter of the Palestinian cause, Daya, like all our ambassadors who chaired the same committee for decades, was strongly critical of Israeli repression in Palestine, as reflected in his reports following visits to Arab capitals.

Perhaps one of his celebrated anecdotes is worth repeating because it was Daya at his best. A week before Daya left Colombo to take up his UN diplomatic assignment back in February 1988, so the story goes, a high-powered delegation from Colombo's nefarious underworld — comprising bookmakers, casino operators and kassippu mudalalis — arrived at his home in Siripa Lane, Thimbirigasaya, at the crack of dawn and greeted him as he returned from his daily morning swim at the SSC pool.

The head honcho of the local mafia delegation scratched his head in characteristic Sri Lankan style and said in home-spun Sinhala: "Sir, we have a small problem." "Why, what's the problem?" asked Daya, as he tried to figure out what crime he was being called upon to defend — this time, on the eve of his departure to New York.

"Sir, we are told you will be away in New York for three years. You have been our only savior, and we really don't know what to do? We don't have anyone else to turn to." Daya contemplated for a while, picked up his thoughts — and his sharp sense of humor — and replied: "My only advise to you is that you suspend all your operations (read: crimes) until I return."

"But when I return," he said, adding the riveting punchline, "mage gastuwa (my legal fees) will double." And so, there were unconfirmed rumours that the crime rate in Colombo had declined during Daya's three-year ambassadorial tenure in New York.

CHAPTER 25

Sri Lanka's Permanent Representative Shirley Hamilton Amerasinghe elected President of the UN General Assembly 1976. Credit: United Nations

When Sri Lanka Presided over the UN's Highest Policy-making Body

At the UN, it was a longstanding tradition for the President of the General Assembly (PGA), the highest policy making body at the UN, to be elected every year on a geographical rotation with each of the member states taking turns (with no member state holding the post more than once, except during the early days of the UN, and with none of the five permanent members of the Security Council running for the post).

Sri Lanka's Permanent Representative Shirley Amerasinghe (1967-78) was elected to that office back in 1976. But when

Foreign Minister ACS Hameed led the first Sri Lanka delegation under the JRJ government, he decided to preside over the Assembly sessions during his one month stay in New York.

But supporters of Shirley were wondering whether Hameed had a right to the presidency when it was Shirley who was elected to the post. So, the Sri Lanka Mission sought a ruling from the UN Office of Legal Affairs which said, irrespective of the individual being elected, the presidency belonged to the country he or she represented. In this case, Sri Lanka. So, in effect, Hameed had the right to preside over the Assembly, which he did for a couple of weeks before he returned home, and the presidency was back in the hands of Shirley until September 1977.

But Shirley's term as ambassador was eventually terminated in 1978 primarily because of a personal feud with President JRJ over negative remarks he had apparently made about JRJ when he was leader of the Opposition. However, when Shirley was unceremoniously ousted from office, he was leading the negotiations at the UN Law of the Sea (LOS) conference which was deciding on an international treaty governing the high seas (United Nations Convention on the Law of the Sea (UNCLOS).

So, when LOS continued its negotiations in Geneva, Shirley had lost his national credentials. Ambassador Neville Kanakaratne, one of outstanding non-career diplomats of his generation, later told me about the crisis of leadership.

And Shirley, a strong supporter of the Palestinian cause and the first chairman of the UN's Israeli Practices Committee, had the backing of Middle Eastern countries. Shirley told Neville that one of the Middle Eastern nations had offered him that country's nationality in order to get the negotiations moving. But Neville told me he had advised him to turn down the offer because Shirley would, in effect, have renounced his Sri Lankan citizenship, in doing so.

The unprecedented crisis was resolved when, perhaps for the first time in the history of the UN, the negotiators decided to keep Shirley as chairman of a UN conference despite the fact he did not have his country's credentials. The vote of confidence on Shirley was interpreted as a resounding slap to the JRJ government.

Incidentally, Shirley's press spokesman during 1976 was a career diplomat, Karen Breckenridge, known to his colleagues as Breck and a movie buff whose favorite line was "Round up the Usual Suspects" from the 1942 Humphrey Bogart movie classic "Casablanca". At one of the daily press briefings, a UN correspondent asked why the Sri Lankan envoy's first name was a female name (best-known names in the US included a movie-star turned US envoy Shirley Temple Black and a Hollywood's iconic actress Shirley MacLaine),

Breck had a ready answer or perhaps concocted one, when he told reporters that Shirley's parents were expecting a baby girl and in anticipation had decided on "Shirley" but kept the name even though they were blessed with a baby boy. Whether this was fact or fiction, nobody knew. But apparently to avoid any misconceptions, Shirley officially added his second name to indicate his gender: Shirley Hamilton Amerasinghe.

Meanwhile, when Daya Perera, who succeeded Shirley more than two decades later, was our UN ambassador (1988-91), I had a perennial battle of wits - – and most of the time, he had the last word. He once dismissed news stories in the Lake House newspapers as largely "bogus". Defending my old establishment, I told him that people in Sri Lanka read the Daily News, at least for its obituaries. And Daya shot back: "Even those obituaries are bogus!".

He was right, at least in one instance, when someone planted a "bogus" political obituary in the Daily News in the 1970s taking a pot shot at the then government in power implicitly accusing the Prime Minister of going authoritarian and violating democratic principles of governance.

The infamous obit read: the DEATH OF D.E.M. O'CRACY, BELOVED HUSBAND OF TRUTH, LOVING FATHER OF L.I. BERTIE, BROTHER OF FAITH, HOPE AND JUSTIA, CORTEGE LEAVING ARALIYA WALAUWA, KOLLUPITIYA.

But despite an in-house investigation, Lake House was unable to track down the prankster (with the obituary later being re-produced in the widely read US monthly Reader's Digest under 'Laughter, the Best Medicine'). The guessing game continued – even though some identified the author of the obit as head of an advertising agency in Colombo.

Speaking of obituaries, an equally memorable story took place in 1976 when a veteran Observer news reporter was assigned the task of interviewing the "average man and woman in the street" – basically to praise a rare achievement: the election of Prime Minister Sirimavo Bandaranaike as the chairman of the Non-Alignment Movement (NAM), the most powerful political coalition at that time. The summit in Colombo that year attracted the largest gathering of world political leaders in the history of Sri Lanka.

The story, with quotes from several men and women, made it to the front page of the newspaper. But a couple of days later, a reader called the editor and alerted him to the fact that all those individuals who sang the praises of Mrs. B were no longer living, but dead.

The names had apparently been taken from the day's obituaries disproving the old saying that dead men (and dead women) tell no tales. When asked for an explanation, the reporter claimed those were the names given by the individuals he interviewed in the streets and at bus stops. The management refused to buy his story – and he was unceremoniously fired.

Meanwhile, at the Sri Lanka Mission to the UN, the Deputy Permanent Representative (DPR) is the second highest-ranking official, mostly with Ambassadorial rank, just below the Permanent Representative (PRUN) in the bureaucratic hierarchy. Back in the late 1970s, there was a widespread rumor that a Sri Lankan academic, with outstanding credentials, was in the running for the post of DPR. So, at a dinner for visiting officials, including the Foreign Secretary, I button-holed the academic and asked him either to confirm or deny the rumor.

He looked at me – and at the visiting officials at the dinner table – and said: "You, mean, you want me to carry these guys bags to the airport!". Perhaps that was part of the job description. There was deafening silence at the dinner table.

CHAPTER 26

President Chandrika Bandaranaike Kumaratunga at a meeting with UN
Secretary-General Boutros Boutros-Ghali (1992-1996) Credit: United Nations

The Only Female Head of State to Address the UN Back in 1998

In September 1998, President Chandrika Bandaranaike Kumaratunga (CBK), to the delight of feminists at the United Nations, was the only female head of state to address the male-dominated UN General Assembly session that year.

But her unique presence also prompted a question from a female CNN reporter who asked her at a UN press conference: "As a woman, and a Head of State, what is your view of the Clinton-Lewinsky affaire?" (President Clinton's much-publicized affair with Monica Lewinsky, a White House intern)

For a moment, the briefing room remained silent. But far from being rattled, the President smiled at the reporter and said it would not be appropriate for her to make any comments. And then, with characteristic diplomacy, she added: "I think it is a matter for the American government and the American public to decide."

When I reported the press conference for the Sunday Times, I pointed out that President Kumaratunga, who is known to be "punctually late" at political and social events at home, surprisingly arrived early for the briefing but was kept waiting for at least 20 minutes because the French Prime Minister overshot his time limit the same press room.

Less than 24 hours earlier, however, the General Assembly had given the embattled Clinton a heart-warming, standing ovation, only the second time it had done so after South African President Nelson Mandela was greeted in similar fashion during his first visit to the UN.

The massive show of international support for President Clinton, which included rousing applause from the Sri Lankan delegation, was a slap in the face to the Republican-controlled US Congress which was not only tightening the screws on the US president but was also in the process of cutting off funding for the United Nations.

At a formal luncheon for heads of state, hosted by Secretary-General Kofi Annan, President Kumaratunga shared a table with both Presidents Clinton and Nelson Mandela. "We had a very long chat," she told reporters. She discussed many things with Mr. Clinton, she said, but specifically zeroed in on a subject worrying both: terrorism.

The speeches made by both presidents had so much in common — particularly on terrorism — that one diplomat wondered whether the similarities were by accident or by design. "Judging by the common theme," one Sri Lankan UN official commented, "I could swear that, maybe, some of our diplomats are also moonlighting for the US State Department or the White House."

Incidentally, just for the record, CBK was the only Sri Lankan head of state who braved reporters at the clubhouse of the UN Correspondents' Association (UNCA) on the third floor of the UN Secretariat. She also agreed to pose for a picture with all the Asian correspondents based at the UN.

In newspaper offices, a similarly posed image would be described as "a firing squad picture". And she asked me: "What is a firing squad picture?" I regretted not telling her that it was more appropriate for LTTE leader Prabakharan than her. The briefing, incidentally, was followed by a reception hosted by the Sri Lanka Mission to the UN—another rare event by a visiting Sri Lankan leader.

Meanwhile, when Lakshman Kadirgamar made his annual visits to the United Nations in the mid-1990s and early 2000s, he used the world body as a platform to continue his intense diplomatic campaign to have the LTTE banned — particularly in the US, the UK and other European countries. And it was also during his tenure as Foreign Minister that the United

Nations gave its collective blessings to his proposal to declare an annual "International Day of Observance for Vesak".

Still, Kadirgamar remained skeptical about the UN — even though it was his primary battleground, as he shunted in and out of closed-door meetings, while holding court in the diplomatic lounge, with an endless parade of foreign ministers.

When I interviewed him at the UN Plaza Hotel back in September 1999, he lambasted the UN for its "humanitarian intervention" in the domestic affairs of member states—and particularly in Sri Lanka.

Since the primary mandate of most UN agencies is socio-economic — including poverty and hunger alleviation, reproductive health, the environment, and healthcare — the foreign minister said the UN would be best advised to "stick to malaria and mosquitoes" — "and leave us to resolve our own political problems."

That was a contemptuous rebuke by someone who once held a senior UN position as head of the Asia Pacific Bureau of the Geneva-based World Intellectual Property Organization (WIPO).

As he pitched into UN officials for shooting their mouths off in public, he dismissed a former UN official, who was based in Colombo, as "a pompous ass" who was told in no uncertain terms where his authority began — and ended.

At a more official level, the former President of the prestigious Oxford Union routinely dispensed with the traditional gesture of meeting with the UN Secretary-General for "photo-ops" —

an annual ritual in New York every September.

Speaking before the UN Correspondents' Association (UNCA) back in 1999, he said the UN really has no mediating role — or for that matter any role at all — in resolving the civil strife in Sri Lanka.

Meanwhile, Gamani Corea, a former Governor of the Central Bank in Sri Lanka and ex-Secretary-General of UNCTAD, was one of the harshest critics of the World Bank and the International Monetary Fund (IMF). Addressing a luncheon at the UN delegates dining room, he castigated the two Bretton Woods institutions for their obsession in laying down stringent conditions – euphemistically called "structural adjustment policies" – in return for concessional loans to the world's poorer nations.

The tragedy of it all, he said, is that virtually all of the crises stricken Third World nations have a common finance minister: the IMF. As if to reaffirm Corea's contention, New York Times columnist Tom Friedman recounted in his book on globalization an anecdote about a newly appointed Indian finance minister being congratulated by a friend. "Don't congratulate me," he tells the friend, "I am only half a minister. My other half is in Washington" (read: IMF).

The IMF's demands from developing nations usually include the removal of state subsidies, privatization of government corporations, downsizing of bureaucracies, devaluation of national currencies, reduction of budgetary deficits, and sharp cuts in military spending and government salaries. In effect, what the IMF says to most developing nations is: If you don't play the game by our rules, you don't get anything from us.

When Prime Minister Ranil Wickremasinghe was in New York to address the UN General Assembly (at a time when our President was both head of state and head of government, according to the constitution), the Sri Lanka Mission to the UN apparently misled the UN Office of General Assembly Affairs and also the Office of Protocol by designating our Prime Minister as head of government (which he was not) and which gave him a prime speaking slot. But when I pointed out this glaring error, I was told: "Well, Ranil had a majority in Parliament, and so, he was the real head of government". But that's one for the constitutionalists…

The scene shifts to Washington DC when a visiting Sri Lankan Prime Minister was trying to get a one-on-one meeting with President Ronald Reagan. But the White House and the State Department, which are extremely protocol conscious, would not relent to that request primarily because our Prime Minister was neither a head of state nor a head of government, according to our then constitution.

As a result, the Prime Minister was offered only "a photo op" to pose for pictures with Reagan. Waiting outside the White House, along with our Prime Minister, were members of the visiting Sri Lankan delegation and several American reporters and photographers.

At the scheduled time, Reagan walked in as the cameras kept clicking almost endlessly. And even though our Prime Minister was advised that it would be only a photo op, he politely asked Reagan whether he could meet with him for a brief discussion. Reagan, who was apparently not pleased with the request, turned to his White House and State Department staffers, and asked: 'What's the meaning of this? I thought this was only a photo op?". And then he turned to our Prime Minister, and in a presidential snub, said: "Mr. Prime Minister, Sorry I am busy" and walked away. Perhaps a bitter lesson in diplomatic protocol.

CHAPTER 27

When the UN Ran Out of Chairs

When Palitha Kohona was Sri Lanka's Permanent Representative to the UN (2009-2015), he was elected as the Chair of the UN General Assembly's Sixth Committee (Legal) in 2013, was Co-Chair of the UN Working Group on Biological Diversity Beyond National Jurisdiction, and inherited two other chairs: Chair of the UN Committee on Israeli Practices in the Occupied Arab Territories (also known as the Israeli Mal-Practices Committee) and chair of the long-defunct UN Ad hoc Committee on the Indian Ocean Zone of Peace. So, when I spoke at this farewell dinner at the Harvard Club in New York, I jokingly told (amid loud laughter from ambassadors and senior UN diplomats), that Palitha chaired so many Committees, that the UN ran out of chairs.

I noticed Palitha's relationship with the then Foreign Minister was visibly different from other diplomats because he addressed his immediate boss by his first name (not the customary "Sir", as all diplomats do, with the exception of

Ambassador Ernest Corea who always addressed Foreign Minister ACS Hameed by his first name "Shahul" because they were friends in a bygone era, with Hameed as a budding politician and Ernest as the editor of the Ceylon Daily News and the Ceylon Observe in the 1960s).

Palitha told me his relationship with the Minister was on a student-professor basis because the Minister was a student when Palitha was a lecturer at the Law College in Hulftsdorp. So, when I interviewed the Minister during the General Assembly sessions, I tried to double-check whether he was in fact, a student in Palitha's class. After pondering for a while, the Foreign Minister quipped: "Yes, that was the only class in which I failed".

When Palitha was Foreign Secretary (2006-2009), I had a well-placed "deep throat" in the bowels of the Foreign Ministry (if one is permitted to mix one's metaphor) who was leaking both confidential and not-so-confidential information to me. But since, as the saying goes, there are two sides to every story, I played back these stories anonymously, both for verification and comments. While confirming most of the stories proving the reliability of my source, he eventually hollered: "Who the hell is leaking all these stories to you?" "I have a deep throat," I shot back, "right under your nose."

When Dr Rohan Perera (2015-2018) first stepped into the United Nations as a delegate back in 1980, he entered the building, accompanied by then Permanent Representative Ambassador Ben Fonseka, "through the UN's revolving door at the main entrance,'" as he once recounted his maiden visit to the world body.

Since then, he was in and out of that "revolving door", literally and metaphorically, for nearly 39 years – first as a delegate, then an advisor, followed by stints as chairman and vice-chairman of several UN committees, vice president of the 193-member UN General Assembly and eventually as Permanent Representative of Sri Lanka to the United Nations.

But one of his most enduring jobs was chairman of the UN Adhoc Committee on Measures to Eliminate International Terrorism, a post to which he was elected in 2000. The day he was elected, the outgoing chair and Canadian Ambassador Philippe Kirsch, patted him on the back and joked: "Congratulations Rohan, you are going to be chairman for life."

And that was a premonition that was proved right. The reason: the UN will never agree on a definition of what constitutes terrorism because one man's terrorist is another man's freedom fighter. The 21-year-old committee, which remains sharply divided, is expected to live for forever – with Rohan as the life-time chair.

As someone rightly remarked: to the Indians, it is the Muslims in Kashmir; to the Russians, it is the Chechens; to the Israelis, it is the Palestinians and vice versa; to the Arabs, it is the Israelis; to the Americans, it is ISIS and Al-Qaeda; and to the Chinese it is Uighurs in Xinjiang Province. And anyone else out there?

Prasad Kariyawasan, who served as our UN ambassador

during 2005-2008 and later as Foreign Secretary, had the distinction of holding office or participating in several UN committees culminating as the chair of the UN Committee on the Protection of the Rights of Migrant Workers.

The chairmanship was all the more important – particularly from a Sri Lankan perspective—because of the nearly two million migrant workers, including undocumented workers, mostly in the Middle East, whose remittances to Sri Lanka constituted the biggest single foreign exchange earner for the country, second only to apparel exports.

Dr Stanley Kalpage, who was our Ambassador during 1991-1994 and a distinguished academic at Peradeniya, was meticulous in his reports to the Foreign Ministry back home. He was known to take down copious notes at closed-door meetings, most of them verbatim. At the 1992 Earth Summit in Rio, where I was reporting for a daily conference newspaper, I waited outside the meeting room, grabbed his notes, made xerox copies, and wrote my exclusive stories – scooping the rest of my colleagues.

When I first met Ambassador Charlie Mahendran ("they call me Charlie because they cannot pronounce Chitambaranathan") outside a UN committee room, he said he was planning pay a "courtesy call" on me. "No, no, no," I responded, "It's the other way around. I will have to pay a courtesy call on you".

During his tenure as Permanent Representative (2002-2004), he was saddled with several non-diplomatic political appointees at the Mission. One of them was a Sinhala -speaking driver who had a driver's license – but was unable to read English road signs. So, whenever Mahendran was invited to a social function, particularly outside New York city boroughs, one of the junior diplomats took him on a drive and guided the driver, who faithfully took down notes in Sinhala.

So, when I invited Mahendran and his wife for dinner at my residence at Burgher Avenue in Staten Island, the driver got lost on a rainy night. A furious Mahendran called me from the backseat of his limo, and I helped guide the driver. The resulting joke was that the driver who translated directions to our house was really looking for a non-existing "Lanci Para".

Incidentally, we lived in what was called the "forgotten borough" of New York City in a relatively isolated Staten Island away from the hustle and bustle of Manhattan. But unlike Manhattan, with just one Sri Lankan restaurant, we were blessed with six restaurants serving hard-to-get delicacies, including hoppers, pittu, lamprais and string hoppers (or as I told my dinner guests at home, "hoppers with strings attached"). Not surprisingly, the restaurants were frequently haunted by our diplomats.

So, when Ambassador Kshenuka Senewiratne and her staff were dining at the Randiwa restaurant, during a visit to Staten Island, she sent me a text message she was in "my hometown". I joked that whenever a Sri Lankan diplomat visited Staten Island, a longstanding protocol demanded they pay homage to me by stopping outside my residence and smashing a couple of coconuts, before proceeding further (as they do outside the Kalutara vihara).

Quick with her repartee, Kshenuha texted me back: "Make sure they don't smash your windows," even though we don't live in a glasshouse. Which reminds me: As the veteran LSSP politician Bernard Soysa once told parliament (in a neat twice to an old cliché): "People living in glass houses should not remove their clothes". Forget throwing stones.

CHAPTER 28

Ambassador Ernest Corea, his wife Indra Corea, and my wife Lucille Deen
in our Staten Island apartment in 1984.
Credit: Steve Zaffarano, Staten Island Advance, February 1984

Getting a Closer Look at the Man
'Inside the Glass House'

By Ernest Corea, former Editor of the Ceylon Daily News
and the Observer & later Sri Lanka's Ambassador to the
United States (1981-86). Re-published from the Sri Lanka
Sunday Times.

"Sunday Times" columnist Thalif Deen and his Inter Press
Service (IPS) colleagues were the centre of attention at the "glass
house" back in May 2009 when journalists, diplomats, UN
officials and other well-wishers celebrated the 45th anniversary

of IPS and the 30th anniversary of its UN Bureau. Deen was a key figure in both.

Two visionaries, an Italian-Argentine economist Roberto Savio, and an Argentine political scientist Pablo Piacentini, launched IPS as a source of "alternative news" initially dispatched by regular mail to media outlets in Europe and Latin America. Few observers would have imagined then that this fledgling effort would develop a global presence and be known as "the world's leading news agency on issues such as development, environment, human rights and civil society." It prides itself on giving "a voice to the voiceless."

An Asian publisher who recognized the potential of IPS in its earliest days was Sri Lanka's Esmond Wickremesinghe. He was so convinced about its future prospects that he even attempted to have IPS set up its regional centre for Asia in Colombo. That initiative was destroyed by bureaucratic inertia. What is interesting, however, is that Deen fortuitously reflects a symbolic continuity between Wickremesinghe and IPS.

Wickremesinghe supported IPS, Deen strengthened the news service as a staff member, and it was Wickremesinghe who inducted Deen into journalism.

Several Sri Lankan journalists have left home for "pastures new" and, in doing so, many have moved into other professions. Among those who stayed in the profession, few if any have reached the same professional heights achieved the same journalistic eminence and received the recognition of his peers as has Deen.

He has been cited twice for excellence in U.N. reporting at the annual awards presentation of the U.N. Correspondents' Association, once leading an IPS reporting team in Brazil, and later sharing the gold medal with Reuters. He has covered UN affairs from the 'seventies and been at almost every major UN conference – on population, human rights, environment, social development, globalization and the Millennium Development Goals – as well as at numerous other international events including summits of the Non-Aligned Movement in Havana and of the Group of 77 in Cartagena, Colombia. His circle of contacts is enormous. It is almost impossible to keep count of his scoops.

He has worked at the IPS UN Bureau for over 25 years and held the post of IPS Regional Director for North America, one of five regional divisions maintained by IPS, and head of its UN Bureau. As the IPS Regional Director for North America, Deen managed a wide swath of journalistic territory. He was required to possess and combine management skills, journalistic flair, and a capacity to maintain a competitive edge. He did. Among journalists in the US who cover world affairs, the position of Bureau chief at the UN is, to use the local term, "to die for".

What kind of a person is this Thalif Deen?

Deen is part of a caring family that remains closely-knit although its members are now separated by distance. When two sets of nephews visited New York, Deen did what most New Yorkers hate to do. He drove them down to Washington and showed his nephews around all the main historical sites in the federal capital, including the refurbished and re-established Newseum which is dedicated solely to the media of yesterday, today, and tomorrow. When driving the second set of nephews to Washington, he also brought along a set of Sri Lankan newspapers and a package of love cake, both for friends who live near Washington, a Sri Lankan couple that he has known for many years. That's the kind of gesture that characterizes his friendship.

He grew up in Hulftsdorp and Borella, two towns that are linked by crime and punishment. Borella was at various times the scene of crimes both petty (such as riding a bicycle with a passenger on its bar) and serious (including the murder at point blank range of a police sergeant). Hulftsdorp was where criminals, when found out, would get their just desserts. As a youngster, Deen spent hours at the Hulftsdorp courts, listening to "learned counsel" say their piece and absorbing a great deal about the structure and style of effective argument in the process. What he absorbed then continues to come through in his writing even now.

Deen is an old boy of Zahira College, as he ceaselessly informs anybody who will listen. An Old Royalist in New York, noticing that Deen had many Royalist friends, asked him (quite stupidly) whether he had become an "honorary Royalist". Deen promptly shot back: "My Royalist friends are now all honorary Zahirians."

He is blessed with a robust sense of humour. He has written, for instance, of how he had spoken at a Zahira College Old

Boys Association dinner (in Colombo) about his old school's legendary reputation for playing over-age students in their sports' teams. The mythical reputation, mostly fictional, had even reached Lake House, he said, and when he asked an editor whether he could assign a reporter to cover Zahira's imminent cricket encounter with Royal, which was expected to be a great game, the editor replied: "I say, Deen, when Royal plays St. Thomas' or when St. Peter's plays St. Joseph's, the parents flock to see their children play. When Zahira plays cricket or rugger, the children go to see their fathers play."

Deen continued to speak in this vein at the dinner. The following Sunday he was delighted to find the then "Sunday Times", the rival to his own paper, the "Observer", commenting that "one of the most entertaining after-dinner speeches we have heard in recent months was made at the Zahira College OBA dinner. The gales of laughter that greeted Deen's stories were proof that we Ceylonese have still not lost the art of laughing at ourselves, and that the big schools still teach the essential quality of cutting ourselves down to size." Those were the days.

From Zahira, Deen went on to the University of Ceylon at Peradeniya where he was a boxer, wrestler, and a bodybuilder. When he left Peradeniya with a degree in economics, the Esmond Wickremesinghe link appeared. Wickremesinghe regularly held recruitment exams at Lake House for new graduates aspiring to be journalists.

Deen did exceptionally well at one of these and Wickremesinghe recruited Deen to the Lake House Economic

Intelligence Unit. Whenever Wickremesinghe was travelling, he assigned Deen to work on the "Observer" until his return. That's where Deen was introduced to roll-up-your-sleeves journalism by two inspiring mentors, Denzil Peiris, the editor and Clarrie Fernando, the news editor.

A Thorough Professional

Denzil was skilled at all branches of journalism, and generously shared his own expertise with younger colleagues. He would frequently urge them to check their facts at least thrice before setting anything down on paper. Similar advice was dinned into Deen at journalism school in New York where a lecturer told his class: "Even if your mother says she loves you, double-check your story."

Clarrie, despite his golden heart, believed that the best way to produce a competent reporter was to be tough with him or her. So, he growled at young reporters, gave them exacting deadlines, and insisted that any news item submitted for publication should be fact perfect, word perfect, and style perfect when it appeared on his desk.

Deen has never explained what compulsion made him move on from the Daily News where he became Deputy News Editor but leave, he did. He worked for a while on the Hong Kong "Standard". As a recipient of a Fulbright scholarship, he was able to earn a master's degree in journalism from New York's highly regarded Columbia University – Barack Obama is also an alumnus.

He then emigrated to New York where he served as a UN Information Officer, and later worked as a defense analyst and editor with Defense Marketing Services and finally Jane's Information Group in Virginia, before surrendering once again to the pull of day-to-day journalism. He joined the staff of the IPS UN Bureau where he has shone like the big, bright lights of New York's Broadway.

As a New York bachelor, Deen lived for many years at Tudor City, an apartment building conveniently located at shouting distance from UN headquarters. His apartment was always open to visiting Sri Lankans, and he cooked for all manner of homesick men and women from Colombo. What he did with tuna straight out of a can would probably have horrified its manufacturers, but it convulsed the gastric juices and satisfied the desires of his Sri Lankan guests.

And then – wham – during an elevator ride at Tudor City, he met Lucille Altamore, a fellow-resident. Not much later, a minister visiting from Colombo asked a Sri Lankan diplomat: "Have you met Deen's girlfriend? He added: "She's a stunner." No doubt, Deen thought so, too, as he fell for all her endearing qualities like a ton of bricks falling off a cliff. Soon, he was informing friends that he and Lucille were to be married.

There was something of a quandary here. Lucille's religious tradition was as strongly Catholic as Deen's religious tradition was profoundly Islamic. So, could the twain ever meet? They were an immensely smart couple, however, and found a way out of the dilemma, arranging a unique wedding ceremony. It took place in a mosque with a Catholic priest and an imam co-officiating. How's that for true diversity?

The anniversary celebrations behind him, Deen will continue to give "a voice to the voiceless" through his own writing and through his journalistic leadership at IPS. That's the kind of person Deen is.

CHAPTER 29

Sharing a joke with President Ronald Reagan at the White House reception and dinner for President J.R. Jayewardene during his state visit to the US in 1984

From a Hoodlum to a Dean

When I heard that my nephew had graduated with a First Class in Physics at Oxford University, I told my wife, Lucille, I received a Third Class in Economics at the University of Ceylon in Peradeniya – only because there was no Fourth. But hopefully, that was compensated for with a "first" I achieved when I gained admission to Columbia University in New York (while some of my friends thought I was going to a University in Bogota, Colombia).

At Peradeniya, it was the prevalent trend among most undergrads to fancy themselves either as Trotskyites,

Communists or Socialists. When asked about my own political leanings, I told one of my professors I was a die-hard Marxist. "But I followed Groucho, not Karl".

I arrived in New York in September 1971 to do my master's degree in Journalism. The letter from Columbia said I was the "first" student from Sri Lanka (then Ceylon) to gain admission to the Graduate School of Journalism. I wrote three essays as mandatory requirements to qualify for admission—one, my life as a journalist, a second essay on my life at Peradeniya, and third, a review of a movie I had recently seen.

I assumed I did creditably well on all three, at a University where admission, I later discovered, was highly competitive. The headline in an article in the London Guardian was a revelation to me: "How elite US schools (read: Columbia) give preference to wealthy and white 'legacy' applicants". I was neither.

But Ivy League universities may not necessarily be what they claim to be, as challenged by William Buckley Jr. Described as an American public intellectual, a biting commentator and founder of the rigidly conservative National Review magazine, Buckley once said: "I'd sooner be governed by the first 2,000 people listed in the Boston telephone directory than by the entire faculty of Harvard University." Mercifully, he did not single out my alma mater, Columbia, where the Faculty parking lot once had a sign, according to unconfirmed rumors, which read: "Reserved for Nobel Prize Winners Only".

That was an offer no prize winner could ignore considering the fact monthly garage parking could be as high as $500 in luxury apartment buildings in Manhattan compared with the purchase of the entire island of Manhattan for $24 from native Americans by Peter Minuit, Dutch colonial governor of New Amsterdam, at a bargain-basement price of a measly 60 guilders in trinkets back in 1626.

But, as for my admission to Columbia, there was one major hurdle to clear. I was told the tuition fees for the academic year 1971-72 was somewhere in the range of $25,000 to $35,000 compared to today's staggering fees of $159,200. Sri Lanka was going through a severe financial crisis in the 1970s, and as a result, it was officially providing only a measly 3 pounds 10 shillings (roughly about $25-$35) for anyone leaving the country, either for studies or on vacation. My chances of getting to New York were zero.

I was, however, advised to apply for a Fulbright grant. But the Director of Information at the US Information Services (USIS) in Colombo told me even though I had gained admission to one of the "finest Ivy league universities" – which I was ignorant of— and regrettably, he said, all Fulbright grants by the State Department had been doled out for the academic year. "We will make a case on your behalf", he said, "but we are not sure whether it will work."

But less than a week later, with prodding from the then Minister of Education Badi-ud-din Mahmud, whom I had known from my days of news reporting on the Observer, I was told the State Department had authorized the grant. I considered myself lucky.

My Fulbright grant, like all such grants, was channeled through the International Institute for Education (IIE), located just across the UN, where I picked up my monthly cheques and free Broadway theatre tickets at least twice or thrice week—one of the many privileges foreign students were entitled to at that time.

I arrived in New York with a degree of trepidation because my colleagues at Lake House, the newspaper office I worked in, cautioned me, perhaps half-jokingly, that Fulbright grants were given only to "half-bright students". Mercifully, it wasn't so.

For starters, I was terrified of the hazards of subway travel and scared of the impending winter weather. When I complained about the weather on my first-ever winter in New York, a wise-cracking friend advised me: "The best remedy is to curl up in bed with a good book – or with someone who has read one".

At the 2012 annual awards dinner hosted by the UN Correspondents' Association (UNCA)

Still, despite my nagging fears about muggings and violence in the subways, I took the liberty to visit Times Square to catch a movie around the third week of my arrival in New York. I was a longtime movie buff and a some-time movie critic on the Observer and relished my two academic courses at

Columbia: Movie Criticism, by Professor Judith Crist, film critic for New York magazine and the History of Film Making by Professor Andrew Sarris, movie critic for the Village Voice. We were a class of about 10 enjoying the privilege of shuttling between screening rooms in the Times Square neighborhood watching previews – in the company of other movie critics—long before the films were released. At least one particular day, I sat through four movies.

So, for starters, I ventured out—all by myself—to see my first movie in New York City. It was a cold wintry evening, and I was wearing a heavy overcoat. As a penny-pinching foreign student, I found that regular movies were cheapest in Times Square – one dollar before 12 noon and $1.75 rest of the day and night (where movies ran round the clock, and where most out-of-town students used to catch a night's sleep in a back seat of the theater saving hotel costs) compared with $3 tickets at the more comfortable theaters (seats with no bugs) on the east side of Manhattan.

And after the movie, I was waiting on the platform of the Times Square subway station around 10 pm to pick up the number one train to the 116th Street/ Columbia University subway station on Broadway. My dorm, International House, was on 120th street and Riverside Drive, a walking distance from Columbia.

As I was waiting for the train, two New York City cops walked up to me, and one of them put his arms around my shoulder and said: "Let's take a walk." I wasn't told why. I mistakenly thought it was American hospitality at its best. We walked a couple of yards, and one of the cops opened a locked door.

At first glimpse, the dimly lit, windowless room was a scene straight out of a Hollywood crime thriller of the 1940s and 50s. There was just one piece of furniture – a long table with a couple of chairs and a light bulb hanging loose over the table. It was reminiscent of a Humphrey Bogart/Edward G. Robinson film noir where the cops took the bad guys to beat the daylights (or was it the s—t?) out of them.

After locking the door, he asked me: "What are your carrying". I instantly figured what it was all about. But conscious of trigger-happy cops, I instinctively put my hands up, gently unbuttoned my heavy overcoat and showed them a folded curved men's umbrella in the upper inside pocket. Perhaps for the cops, looking at my bulging overcoat, it resembled a folding submachine gun. The cop looked at me and blurted out a warning: "Don't carry your umbrella like that – ever again".

As a footnote, when I returned home to Sri Lanka after graduation, Fred Grayson, the head of my host family in New York and an editor at Simon and Schuster, jokingly asked me in one of his letters: "How is your .45 caliber umbrella?"

As part of my subjects at Columbia, I opted for a one-month academic course on newsgathering where I would spend time with editors at the New York Times (NYT) sitting-in at editorial meetings where decisions were made on which news stories to cover. So, as advised, I called the NYT and sought an appointment with one of the editors to work out the arrangements.

On the appointed day, I arrived at the NYT office and introduced myself to the secretary outside the editor's office. Perhaps there was a breakdown in communication somewhere down the line because the editor rushed towards me, extended his palm, and asked: "You are the Dean of which school at Columbia?" "No, no, no," I said, "I am not a Dean. I am only a student, and my last name is Deen." We both stood embarrassed.

A couple of weeks later, I wrote a piece for a student newspaper run by the Asia Foundation in San Francisco. They ran the story with the headline: 'FROM A HOODLUM TO A DEAN'. I picked up $200 bucks for the story. A lot of moolah for a cash-starved student those days.

After graduation, I spent another year in New York after I won a Journalism Fellowship at International House, my dorm at 500 Riverside Drive, which was home to over 300 students, mostly non-Americans. I was editor of the monthly in-house magazine during 1972-73. In return, I received free board and lodging.

In the mid-1970s after I returned to New York as a permanent resident with a green card, and following a short spell in Sri Lanka and Hongkong, I worked on an 11-month contract as an Information Officer at the UN Secretariat, and later as a Senior Defense Analyst and Director, Foreign Military Markets at Defense Marketing Services (DMS) housed in an isolated, leafy neighborhood in Greenwich, Connecticut.

We had a staff of about 50, most of them retirees or early retirees from the CIA, the DIA (Defense Intelligence Agency), the Pentagon, the US army, Navy, Air Force and the Marine Corps. At 37, I was one of the youngest. Both my academic and UN credentials were a plus, plus.

We were primarily monitoring arms sales throughout the world and publishing politically and militarily-sensitive monthly reports on US weapons systems, including fighter aircraft, combat helicopters, drones, missiles, warships, battle tanks, artillery and electronic warfare, plus political, economic and military profiles of over 150 countries—much of the information available in the public domain, including the annual CIA Factbook, the Military Balance published by the International Institute for Strategic Studies (IISS) and the Annual Yearbook published by the Stockholm International Peace Research Institute (SIPRI).

However, the latest figures for US Foreign Military Sales (FMS), Military Credits, Military Assistance Programs (MAP) and International Military Education and Training (IMET) Programs came from the annual "Congressional Budget Justification – Department of State, Foreign Operations, and Related Programs" (information available in the public domain and submitted annually by the State Department to the US Congress).

Although the company was fully owned by employees, there were widespread rumors we were a front for the CIA or a clandestine CIA op, primarily because of the nature of our work. The scenario was reminiscent of the 1975 political thriller "Three Days of the Condor", about a CIA analyst in a defense research company, played by Robert Redford and code-named Condor, who comes back from lunch one day to discover all his seven co-workers shot to death: a hit job by the CIA on a rogue operation gone awry. The movie was the topic of discussion at the water cooler in our office.

Mercifully, we were spared Redford's tragedy, as he was pursued by a CIA hitman right to the end of the movie. I remember watching the final sequence being shot outside the offices of the New York Times in mid-town Manhattan. Redford walks out of the Times office where his CIA handler, Cliff Robertson, waits for him on the street. When Redford tells Robertson that he has given his entire story on the clandestine CIA operation to the Times, the movie ends with a curtain line from Robertson: "What makes you think they are going to publish it?," triggering the question: Had the CIA infiltrated the NYT?

Meanwhile, our President at Defense Marketing Services, once told the staff he had a call from the CIA asking why we were selling our publications to the Soviets at the height of the Cold War-era—even though our clients were largely hundreds of military contractors and sub-contractors, including General Dynamics, Grumman, Lockheed Martin, Bell Helicopters, Raytheon, plus defense ministries worldwide and think tanks. "Check your client list," the CIA official told our President "because the UN Library was one of your clients – but when the subscription expired, a Russian employee in the Library renewed the subscription with his own personal cheque". And the CIA was dead on target. We cancelled that subscription.

In my days – and nights— both on and off the Columbia campus, and at my dorm at International House, there was never a weekend without "BYOB". That's an acronym for Bring Your Own Booze. When I told one of my friends that BYOB does not resonate with me because I never drank hard liquor, beer or even wine – in my lifetime (and the only beer I drank was ginger beer). That's ok, he replied. "To you, BYOB means Bring Your Own Blonde or Bring your Own Brunette". No redheads.

Unlike Sri Lanka, I realized that Americans were obsessed with first names, and hardly anyone was addressed either by his or her last name or even by initials (one exception was OJ Simpson, known universally as OJ or Orange Juice).

My byline during my reporting days in Sri Lanka was "T.M. Deen, which I continued in my early days at Columbia until a professor who kept addressing me as "TM", queried: "TM, what is your first name?"

And I told him: "Professor, I have only one name, DEEN because my parents couldn't afford more."

"That's a good one", he said as he laughed it off.

And that's when I started using "Thalif" as my first name. Coming from a country with jaw-breaking last names, I was glad that my last name was a four-letter word!

Like most Sri Lankans of Malay ancestry, my first name

was Tuan (although I was known as Dino during my ten years on the afternoon newspaper "The Ceylon Observer" where shoe-leather journalism prompted me to pound the streets of Colombo and Pettah searching for stories on my trade and commerce beat).

The 1965 movie "Lord Jim," based on a Joseph Conrad novel and shot on location in Cambodia, Hong Kong, and Malaysia, played in a theater in Colombo. In the movie, the natives in a remote village in Malaysia bestow the title of "Tuan" on Peter O'Toole, translated to mean "Lord".

In a constant battle of wits with M. Edwards, one of the gifted feature writers on the "Observer", who would always get the better of me, and whose writing style was reminiscent of James Hadley Chase and Damon Runyon, I once jokingly told him, "Don't mess with me. I am a Tuan, and I am a Lord".

And he shot back with a zinger: "I say, if all the Tuans are Lords, the House of Lords should be located in Slave Island, not in the UK."

And Slave Island was a predominantly Malay neighborhood in Colombo with hundreds of Tuans, with at least one street called Java Lane and another Malay Street. Speaking of ancestry, I told my friends in New York that I was half-Malay and half-Moor –and that my upper half was Malay and my lower half Moor.

CHAPTER 30

Standing at the UN General Assembly podium
during an April 1st non-event

A Journalist, Once "Distinguished,"
Now Extinguished

After nearly ten years as a columnist, cranking out weekly pieces for the Sunday Times titled "Inside the Glass House," I decided to call it quits back in December 2008 while continuing my journalistic career as the UN Bureau Chief for Inter Press Service (IPS) news agency.

Having authored over 450 weekly columns, I told the editor, Sinha Ratnatunga, I was going into a "semi-retirement" mode and was looking for a graceful exit strategy while the going was still good. I am not sure whether I convinced Sinha, but I did tell him that no one in this world is indispensable – not even journalists. And as former French President Charles de Gaulle once said in a timeless remark: "The world's cemeteries are full of indispensable people."

I was a journalist at a time and age when there was no answer to the rhetorical question facing newspapermen worldwide: "Is journalism worth dying for?" – whether in Syria, Afghanistan, Iraq, Yemen, Libya, Pakistan, or Sri Lanka. The journalistic awards for some foreign correspondents, specifically in the world's battle zones, arrive long after they have vanished from the face of the earth.

When I was in Iraq during the 1990 Gulf War, I was armed with a military flak jacket with a cautious warning inscribed on the back: "Press. Don't Shoot." Perhaps it helped. Now, I occasionally wear it in the mean streets of New York, a city where I have lived for over 45 years, and where a bank robber, they say, can get mugged as he flees to a get-a-way car.

Having travelled to more than 50 countries, mostly on journalistic assignments, covering UN meetings and international conferences –- from Rio and Rome, to Havana and Harare - I had the privilege of reporting from several cities and capitals, including Cairo, Vienna, Copenhagen, Oslo, Stockholm (12 times), Brussels, The Hague, H elsinki, Caracas, Cartagena, Sao Paulo, Amman, San Jose, Baghdad, Basra, Kuwait City, Abu Dhabi Beirut, Doha, Nairobi, Manila, Reykjavik, Florence, Seoul and Tokyo –- among others.

But since I have cultivated the ability to laugh at myself,

I recount the words of Tom Stoppard in "Night and Day," a play on post-colonial politics and journalism when he took a passing shot at roving journalists. "A foreign correspondent", he said, "is someone who flies around from hotel to hotel (five or four-star?) and thinks the most interesting thing about any story is the fact that he has arrived to cover it". If that does not deflate roving correspondents worldwide, what would?

I may have semi-retired from the Sunday Times, but I remained active at the IPS UN Bureau (www.ipsnews.net) which is over 56 years old. In reality, journalists rarely retire. And these days, they probably die with their laptops and their I-Pads on. Forget boots. At her 84th birthday celebrations, a woman editor of a New York-based magazine was asked when she plans to retire. Her response: "I am too old to retire." So am I.

Having covered the UN since my student days at Columbia University in the early 1970s, I never considered myself an authority on any subject relating either to the UN or international politics. I realized I learn something new every day.

Ambassador H.M.G.S. Palihakkara, a sharply-witty former Foreign Secretary and a one-time Permanent Representative to the UN, once paid a compliment, perhaps back-handed, when he said in an email message: "Permanent representatives are never permanent. Sri Lanka's only Permanent Representative at the UN is the IPS UN Bureau Chief Thalif Deen."

He said I had survived about 20 Permanent Representatives

(PRUNs) – perhaps some of them transiting through New York, as politics transcend professionalism in Sri Lanka's foreign service.

While doing a course on International Reporting at Columbia, I was filing stories for the Daily News and the Observer with a United Nations dateline. Among them were several stories critical of the failed efforts in by the US in late 1971 to prevent the ouster of the Republic of China (Taiwan) from the UN and its replacement by the People's Republic of China.

I received a note of warning from a Sri Lankan journalist with contacts in the American Embassy in Colombo. I was told copies of my articles were produced at a Monday morning staff meeting where one of the diplomats said: "We sent this guy on a Fulbright grant – and see what he is writing." But it certainly did not cramp my style.

Meanwhile, after the US invasion of Iraq in March 2003, I wrote a series of articles strongly critical of the foreign policy of the Bush administration. The articles obviously irritated the then US Ambassador in Colombo Jeffrey Lunstead who fired off a confidential cable to the State Department in Washington

A member of the Sri Lanka delegation to the UN General Assembly sessions in 1978.

producing verbatim one of my articles titled "US Bogged Down in Iraq, Crawls Back to UN" (published in the Sunday Times in 2004).

Lunstead's cable, revealed subsequently by Wikileaks, described my article as "resolutely anti-American" and "a virulent attack on US policy in Iraq." Still, the American ambassador was constrained to admit in his cable that the Wijeya Group, which publishes the Sunday Times, is "among the most respected newspaper groups" in Sri Lanka.

As is well known, newspapermen around the world, including in the US, are closely monitored both by democratic governments and also by repressive regimes. Just after the 9/11 attacks in the US on 11 September 2001, two agents of the Federal Bureau of Investigation (FBI) visited my neighbors to check my credentials – possibly to find out whether, as a journalist, I was a "good Muslim or a bad Muslim" by American standards.

If they checked my files (the FBI and CIA maintain such files on virtually all journalists here), the FBI agents would have discovered that I hold an American passport; worked as a military analyst at Defense Marketing Services (once wrongfully accused of having ties to the CIA); married an Italian-American (whose family, my friends joke, is linked to the Mafia in Calabria, Italy); and in a wedding ceremony held in a New York City mosque officiated by an Egyptian imam.

At the John F. Kennedy airport after the 9/11 attacks, at a time of widespread racial profiling, one of the security officers confiscated my razor, probably assuming it could be used as a dangerous weapon, which was in my hand-carrying luggage when II embarked on a flight to Europe.

I looked at him and said with a mischievous smile: "You take my razor from me. And if I grow a beard, you call me an Islamic fundamentalist. Either way, I lose."

Meanwhile, in early October 1971. I found myself an uninvited guest at the historic inaugural meeting of the Sri Lanka Association of New York (SLANY), the first such organization of Lankan expatriates in the US at that time. I was there by sheer accident, not by design.

The Association made a world of difference – bo th b me, as a newly-arrived, home-sick student, and to scores of pioneering expatriates, mostly original settlers in the US, who were seeking out their compatriots in the tri-state area of New York-New Jersey-Connecticut in the early 1970s.

That isolation was aggravated by the fact that I was single —while most expats arrived with their wives. My mother did warn me that I should take a wife along with me, but I told her, in typical home-spun idiom, that taking a woman to New York was like carrying rambutans to Malwana – or carrying coals to Newcastle.

The early history of SLANY, which has survived for 50 long years, would not be complete without the multiple anecdotes which were widespread in the community. As a newspaperman doubling as a raconteur, I was quick to pick them up.

Meanwhile, one of the stories, as recalled by expatriates

who landed in the shores of this country in the early 1950s, was that even the Sri Lanka Mission to the UN was so woefully understaffed they were desperately looking for Lankans to boost the delegation to the annual General Assembly sessions, September through December.

According to one anecdote, Sri Lankan diplomats were seen hanging around the corner of First Avenue and 42nd Street, right across from the UN building, determined to grab the first Lankan who crossed the street – and forcibly anoint him a member of our delegation.

But no longer. Judging by our recent performances, we now have an oversupply of delegates to New York every year, including ministers, MPs, career diplomats, security officers, masseurs and even hairdressers.

And as the only accredited New York and UN correspondent for the Ceylon "Daily News" and the "Sunday Observer" in the 1970s, I provided extensive coverage – the positive, the negative and the hilarious — because there was never a dull moment in the formative years of the Association.

When SLANY hosted its first Sri Lanka New Year in 1977, I filed a story for the Sunday Observer which ran with the headline: KIRIBATH AND LUNU MIRIS IN NEW YORK. When the validity of the SLANY elections was challenged in a court of law in 1979, the headline read: "HORA VOTES" BY LANKANS IN USA. The "hora votes" was a direct quote attributed to a former SLANY secretary who filed the legal challenge because of allegations of ballot-stuffing at the elections.

And when two expatriates were engaged in a bout of fisticuffs, beating the daylights out of each other, at an annual general meeting at a school auditorium in the Bronx, a New York City borough, the lead paragraph in my news story read: "When Sri Lankans want to enjoy some fun and frolic, they either go to the Barnum & Bailey circus at Madison Square Garden or the annual general meeting of SLANY – whichever comes first."

Meanwhile, a one-time SLANY President, Sydney Silva, gifted with a sense of humor, told a stunned gathering of Lankans at the annual Summer Festival in Denville, New Jersey, that two of the distinguished patrons of SLANY, both ambassadors, along with the president of SLANY, were "gays". And seconds later, he delivered the punch line when he said they were "gays" – not in the American sense but in the Sri Lankan sense, as he singled out, amidst loud laughter, the three "gays" as LIYANA-GE, GURU-GE AND KALPA-GE.

Jay Liyanage was the legendary President of SLANY, Dr Ananda Guruge was a Buddhist scholar, a civil servant, and our ambassador to the US while Dr Stanley Kalpage was Sri Lanka's Permanent Representative to the UN, a distinguished Professor at Peradeniya University and Warden of Marrs Hall, where I spent four years as a resident undergrad. They were both Patrons of SLANY.

When SLANY was born, it had three primary goals: promoting and fostering social and cultural activities; presenting a proper image before the American public and providing advice and assistance to any incoming Sri Lankans (of which I was one of the beneficiaries).

There was only a single Sri Lankan restaurant in mid-town Manhattan— the "Ceylon-India Inn" – but unaffordable to students like me, even as I refused to eat "hamburgers" erroneously thinking it had "ham" in it. I fancied myself "Jewish" for not eating pork because "Muslims" and "halal food" were perhaps never heard of at that time. If cheeseburgers had cheese, why shouldn't hamburgers have ham? A logical question for a newly arrived in New York.

But all that changed dramatically with the birth of SLANY when I cultivated new friendships—and found myself invited to rice-and-curry family dinners on weekends. Meanwhile, the links between SLANY and the United Nations were exceptionally strong. The Association was born in the shadow of the UN, and the first meeting was held at the Sri Lanka mission to the UN on Third Avenue and 40th street.

In his message to SLANY back in December 1996, Jayantha Dhanapala, a former Ambassador and UN Under-Secretary-General, very appropriately quoted President Abraham Lincoln, who famously said: "Never consider an immigrant to become a loyal American citizen unless he retains his love for his motherland."

And rightly so.

ABOUT THE AUTHOR

Thalif Deen, a former UN Bureau Chief and Regional Director at Inter Press Service (IPS) news agency, is a Fulbright scholar with a master's degree (MSc) in Journalism from Columbia University, New York.

A former Deputy News Editor at the Ceylon Daily News and Senior Editorial Writer on the Hong Kong Standard, he once served as Information Officer at the UN Secretariat. He was twice a member of the Sri Lanka delegation to the General Assembly sessions. He has been cited for excellence in UN reporting at the UN Correspondents' Association (UNCA) annual awards presentation and shared the first prize, the prestigious gold medal, in two consecutive years: 2012 and 2013.

In his stint as a military analyst, he was Director, Foreign Military Markets at Defense Marketing Services; Senior Defense Analyst at Forecast International; and military editor Middle East/Africa at Jane's Information Group. He was also a longstanding columnist for the Sri Lanka Sunday Times, UN correspondent for Asiaweek, Hong Kong and Jane's Defense Weekly, London.

ACKNOWLEDGEMENTS

I owe a deep debt of gratitude to Rod Grigson, a longstanding friend and published author, who worked with me at the United Nations back in the 1970s and '80s. This book would have remained unceremoniously buried inside my desktop computer – and would never have reached a publisher – if not for his magnanimous support and superlative guidance from Down Under.

Rod went on to serve with the UN Peace Keeping Forces in the Middle East and was a part of the team that developed and implemented word processing in six languages across the UN system. He migrated in the late '80s to Melbourne, Australia with his wife Mena, who also worked with us at the UN.

After attaining the position of Vice President of a prestigious global networking company, a position he held for several years, Rod retired at an early age and began his writing career, publishing three books (www.rodericgrigson.com) and becoming a Creative Writing teacher and book publishing specialist.

Having first met in Ceylon (now Sri Lanka), the two of us lived in New York when it was known as 'Sin City'. New York in the early 1970s was not the New York of today. It was a city compelling in its contradictions: a vibrant and cheap place to live in while it attracted talented young people from all over the world in droves. Known as the world's financial and entertainment capital, it was also bursting at the seams.

'Stay away from New York City if you possibly can' was the blunt warning that greeted visitors at New York city's airports, courtesy of a mysterious 'survival guide' with a hooded death's head on the cover that symbolized one of the weirdest and most turbulent periods in the city's history. This was the place the two of us navigated, enjoying the life the most dangerous city in the world had to offer.

Which reminds me of a cartoon in the Wall Street Journal depicting a family living in a tree-top jungle habitat where the mother says goodbye to her son venturing out for his studies for the first time in the big city. "And be careful," she warns the son, "it's a jungle out there".

And we lived in that asphalt jungle called New York – and survived to tell the tale.

I would also like to extend my thanks to my nephew Feroz Deen who is continuing the family tradition, this time in broadcast journalism. As the Channel Head at E 88.3FM radio station in Sri Lanka, he was always quick to provide me with technical assistance and guidance thousands of miles away from New York City.

Made in the USA
Monee, IL
25 February 2021